Mankato Milestones
1852-2002

The Historians' Handbook of Facts and Folklore
from the Mankato Area

Bryce O. Stenzel

Minnesota Heritage Publishing
Mankato, Minnesota
@2002
The Year of the Sesquicentennial

Copyright © 2001 Minnesota Heritage Publishing and Bryce O. Stenzel
All rights reserved.
Reproduction in whole or in part of any portion in any form
without permission of the author or publisher is prohibited.
For more information, write to Minnesota Heritage Publishing,
205 Ledlie Lane, Suite 125, Mankato, MN 56001
www.mnheritage.com

ISBN: 0-9713168-1-3

Library of Congress Catalog Number: 2002102456

Published by Minnesota Heritage Publishing

Printed in the United States of America
By Corporate Graphics, North Mankato, MN

First Edition

Edited by Julie A. Schrader

Cover: The Official Sesquicentennial Print, "The First 150 Years,"
by Mankato Artist, Marian Anderson.
For more information contact: Marian Anderson Gallery,
20101 Horseshoe Lane, Mankato, MN 56001.

This Book is Dedicated to the People of Mankato, Past, Present and Future.

About the Author

Bryce Stenzel was born and raised in rural Mankato, Minnesota. As a boy, he learned to appreciate the unique history of his hometown. The stories he absorbed as a child left such an impression on him that, by the time he graduated from high school in 1986, Stenzel resolved to become a professional historian. Stenzel attended Mankato State University, where he earned his Bachelor of Science in Teaching Degree in 1990 and his Master of Arts Degree in History in 1995. Stenzel's first book, *Abraham Lincoln: Man of the People* was published in 1996, by the Friends of the Minnesota Valley Regional Library. In addition to this book, Minnesota Heritage Publishing will be releasing another of Stenzel's works in 2002, *German Immigration to the Minnesota River Valley Frontier, 1852-1865: Wir Stammten aus Deutschland nach Hausen Minnesota.*

About the Book Cover

"The First 150 Years"

by Marian Anderson

When I started this painting, I wanted to express the progress of 150 years. I started at the bottom of the canvas and worked upward; depicting the passage of time.

1852 begins with the tall prairie grass, limestone outcroppings and the bend of the Minnesota River. You will notice the spirits of the Native Americans. Placed at the bend in the river is the steam paddleboat, which was the first means of bringing people and materials to the new settlement. The early pioneers are remembered by the couple walking into the sunlight and the promise of a new future. Many other settlers arrived by stagecoach. Later, the train replaced the paddleboats, bringing more settlers and supplies for the town to grow and develop.

Placed in the heart of the painting is an hourglass, indicating time. The book, *The History of the Minnesota Valley*, is a respected book, most preferred by historians wishing to learn about the settlement and history of this area.

There is a faint image of the streets of Mankato, as they were in the flourishing beginnings of the town. You can recognize the streetcars that used to operate in the streets of Mankato and the horse-drawn wagons.

The maple leaf represents two things, the passage of seasons and the beauty of the Minnesota Valley. Mingled lightly, you can detect an outline of Betsy, Tacy and Tib in memory of Mankato author, Maud Hart Lovelace. She is best known for her children's books, written about growing up in Mankato— Lovelace's fictional "*Deep Valley*."

To the right of the picture is the First National Bank, which still exists as part of the Midwest Wireless Civic Center, and represents the wealth of the community. Above the bank is Hubbard Milling, now Cargill, which represents industry. St. Peter and Paul's Catholic Church brings attention to all faiths of the community, and Old Main represents education.

Front Street was painted as it was in the late 1960s, as many relish the memory of the old downtown. Entertainment is recalled by the three downtown theaters: the Grand, Town and State. Fine dining of the time is remembered by a sign for Michaels'.

Many years were enjoyed shopping at Madison East and now River Hills Mall. As we progress to the future, we are reminded of time by the clock tower at the Minnesota State University campus. The Taylor Center, Midwest Wireless and the Intergovernmental Center remind us of the present.

The Lady of Justice from atop the courthouse holds the balance of all times. A vacant space, at the top left, represents future development. It is enhanced by today's street light and the Mankato banner as a symbol of hope for the future and respected memory of our forefathers. Lightly sketched is Amos Owen, who cannot be forgotten for his effort to bring reconciliation. The centennial edition of the *Free Press* shows the daily recording of the events of our era. The Main Street Bridge depicts the togetherness of the community.

How to Use This Book

This book is arranged in a question and answer format and is divided into decades.

Each decade begins with a list of numbered questions or statements of inquiry pertaining to a historical topic. Each commentary is numbered to correspond with these and is found following the question or statement of inquiry section for that decade. The commentary pages are tabbed at the edge of the page by a gray shaded bar to make it easier for the reader to locate.

Table of Contents

Preface ix
1850s 1
1860s 11
1870s 21
1880s 27
1890s 33
1900s 39
1910s 45
1920s 51
1930s 59
1940s 65
1950s 71
1960s 77
1970s 83
1980s 89
1990s 95
2000-2002 101

Appendix 105
    Minnesota River Steamboats 107
    Coming to Terms with the Past 111
Bibliography 113
Index 117

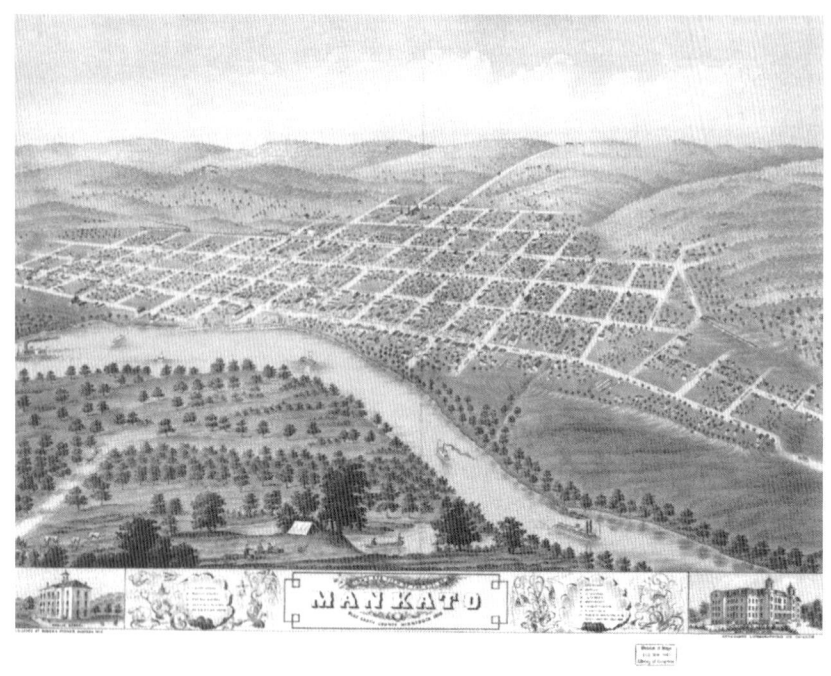

Popular in the nineteenth and early twentieth centuries, panoramic or "bird's-eye view" maps were non-photographic representations of U.S. and Canadian cities, portrayed as if viewed from above at an oblique angle. Generally, they were not drawn to scale; however, they depicted street patterns, individual buildings and major landscape features in perspective. Post-Civil War town views, such as this one of Mankato, published in 1870, were more accurate. They were drawn from a higher oblique angle than earlier panoramic maps, done in the modified "Renaissance city view" style of cartography.

Preface

Pierre Charles LeSueur, a French fur trader and explorer was usually credited as being the first European to lay his eyes on the confluence of the Blue Earth and Minnesota Rivers, deep in the heart of the Santee (Eastern) Dakota territory. Although the wooden stockade (Fort L'Huillier) he built nearby has long since disintegrated and disappeared, LeSueur's presence was preserved through his naming of geographic features: LeSueur River, LeHillier, St. Pierre's River (Minnesota) and most notably, his recording of the Dakota name for blue earth—"mahkato" or "mankato."

One hundred and fifty years after LeSueur's visit in 1700, another group of pioneers came to the confluence of the two rivers. Unlike LeSueur, Nicollet, Carver and the other explorers who came to the wilderness to trade directly with the Indians, these Americans came to settle permanently, and in doing so significantly altered the geographic landscape. Parsons King Johnson and Henry Jackson built a townsite providing settlers with finished goods as well as an outlet for their raw materials. Business flourished. The name chosen for the townsite was "Mankato."

The name for the town was appropriate because it demonstrated recognition by the founders of the important role rivers played in the development of a community. Rivers were the superhighways of their time, bringing people and goods closer together. Eventually, railroads and highways replaced the waterways as the primary means of transportation, but the Minnesota and the Blue Earth Rivers remained forces to be reckoned with.

The original plan for the townsite of Mankato called for laying out its center at the confluence of the two rivers. Realizing that severe flooding was likely, the town fathers wisely chose to relocate the town's center several miles downstream at the great bend of the Minnesota River where it has been ever since. Even then there were periodic floods, as anyone alive in 1951, 1965, 1993 or 1997 can testify. Such calamities resulted in the construction of a concrete floodwall in the 1970s as a means of keeping the Minnesota River and its tributaries in check.

Living with the rivers has formed a key component of Mankato's character as a city. Even the unique street pattern of the downtown area, in which a street suddenly changes direction while appearing to be straight, was a result of the town being built at the bend of the Minnesota River. Originally, streets were numbered up from the Minnesota River, beginning with "Front" Street instead of "First." What should have been designated "Third" Street was given the name "Broad." These facts alone would not be that interesting, but there was the story of the foreign traveler who avoided getting lost anywhere on his journey across the United States until he arrived in Mankato only to become hopelessly confused by one street having as many as three names: "Front," "Park Lane" and "Minneopa Road." Later it was decided to rename the street "Riverfront" in an attempt to remove the confusion. However, the problem still persisted with there being a "Front Street" along with the new "Riverfront" Street.

There are many such stories and bits of folklore about Mankato people, places and events. Together, they have formed a rich tapestry of history for this community. It is the sincere hope of the author that this book of facts and folklore, written in trivia question format, will both enhance the reader's appreciation for the area's history as well as provide them with a quality keepsake from the Mankato Sesquicentennial celebration for many years to come.

Efforts have been made to ensure the historical accuracy of the book's content, by presenting it in a scholarly manner, with the use of citations. At the same time, it was the author's desire to bring the rich history of Mankato alive to the general reader. There was no way to include every business, individual or event from the past 150 years in this book. Rather, efforts were made to use specific examples to represent common themes in Mankato's historical development. Any omissions or oversights, while not intentional, are the author's responsibility.

—BOS

The Ott Cabin was built by George Ott in 1857. In 1931, the cabin was moved to its present location in Sibley Park to mark the site of Henry Sibley's trading post, for whom the park was named.

"Favorite" at Mankato Levee, 1863.
The steamboat "Favorite" was one of many vessels that plied the waters of the Minnesota River during the steamboat era (1850-1897). It gained lasting notoriety for its role in transporting the remaining Dakota Indian prisoners from Mankato to Fort Snelling, in the aftermath of the Dakota Conflict of 1862.

1850s

1) What was the name of the first steamboat to travel on the Minnesota River in 1850?

2) Which treaty was signed between whites and Indians near St. Peter in 1851?

3) Mankato was first settled in what month and year?

4) Who built the first log cabin in Mankato?

5) Who were Mankato's "founding fathers?"

6) Who came up with the name "Mankato?"

7) What did the name "Mankato" mean?

8) Who were the original inhabitants of the Mankato area?

9) Where was the center of the original townsite located?

10) Why was the townsite relocated?

11) What was the Native American name given to the river that Mankato was built beside?

12) What was the European name originally given to the same river?

13) Where did Mankato's founders come from?

14) What were their occupations?

15) What means of transportation was used to bring the first settlers to Mankato?

16) When did the Dodd Road first open?

17) What was the significance of this road?

18) Name Mankato's first hotel built in 1853.

19) What distinction did Mankato receive in 1854?

20) What was one of Mankato's earliest industries that is still in operation in 2002?

21) This townsite was platted in 1853 and rivaled Mankato.

22) What were the first religious congregations established in Mankato in the 1850s?

23) What was the name given to Mankato's first public school, organized in 1855?

24) What Indian tribe was moved to its new reservation in Blue Earth and Waseca counties, in the 1850's?

25) Beginning in 1856, Parsons King Johnson served as Mankato's first?

26) Who was the first-known physician to arrive in Mankato in 1856?

27) This existing building on North Riverfront Street housed one of the earliest saloons in Mankato in the 1850s.

28) What was the significance of the Spirit Lake Massacre of 1857 on Mankato?

29) Why was the townsite of Mankato built so close to a major river?

30) What was Mankato's first newspaper?

31) What was Mankato's first brewery?

32) When did Minnesota become a state?

33) What was first held in 1859 and is one of Minnesota's oldest?

34) Who opened a harness-making shop on Hickory Street, between Front and Second Streets in 1859?

Answers and Commentary, 1850s

1) The *Anthony Wayne* was the first steamboat to travel on the Minnesota River. In the early summer of 1850, Captain Able brought his steamboat up the Mississippi River from St. Louis and docked in St. Paul. He had long dreamed of taking his boat upstream on the Minnesota River, southwest of Fort Snelling; but until this point, no one had attempted such a feat. The Minnesota River was notorious for its sandbars and tree snags that could severely damage a steamboat or send it to the bottom. With the urging of some of his passengers, Captain Able decided to make an attempt. In his first trip, the *Anthony Wayne* made it as far upstream on the Minnesota as the present town of Carver. Later that summer, Able tried again; this time he made it as far as three miles south of the present town of Mankato. It was on this second trip that Parsons King Johnson and Henry Jackson caught their first glimpse of the location of their future townsite.[1]

In his *History of the Minnesota Valley*, the Reverend Edward D. Neill recounted the story differently. According to his account, Johnson was aboard the excursion steamboat *Yankee*, when he first laid eyes on the future townsite of Mankato. There was no mention of Jackson being present.[2] The *Yankee* made its trip up the Minnesota River one week after the *Anthony Wayne* made its second voyage. Neill's dates were precise, the *Anthony Wayne* made its first trip in June 1850. The second trip was begun on July 18. The *Yankee* sailed on July 22, taking advantage of the unusually high water that year.[3]

2) There were two treaties signed between whites and Indians in 1851. The one signed near St. Peter on July 23, 1851, was the Treaty of Traverse des Sioux. The other treaty, signed in early August, was the Treaty of Mendota. Altogether, over 24,000,000 acres of land were ceded by the Indians to the United States government in exchange for two reservations along the Minnesota River and $3,075,000 in cash and annuities over a span of fifty years. Each reservation was approximately seven miles long and twenty-five miles wide. It was the violation of these treaty obligations on the part of the U. S. government, as well as

---

[1] Mabel Ulrich, John G. Rockwell and Parker T. Van de Mark, Minnesota County Histories Series: Blue Earth County, (Minnesota Federal Writers' Project, 1938), 11-12.

[2] Edward D. Neill and Charles S. Bryant, History of the Minnesota Valley, Including the Explorers and Pioneers of Minnesota and History of the Sioux Massacre, (Minneapolis: North Star Publishing Company, 1882), 537.

[3] Ibid., 165.

the government's failure to supervise the activities of its Indian Agents and traders that led to the Dakota Conflict of 1862.[4]

3) Mankato was founded on February 5-6, 1852. Johnson arrived at the confluence of the Blue Earth and Minnesota Rivers on February 5 and camped at Sibley Mound that night. It had been named "Sibley Mound" in honor of Henry Hastings Sibley, who had operated a trading post there some years before. The next day, he and the rest of the party, consisting of three other men, went exploring and decided to relocate their campsite to the vicinity of where the Masonic Temple now stands. DeMoreau, the French teamster, returned to St. Paul for a load of provisions. The others began building a log cabin.

4) Hiram Fuller. He arrived with Parsons King Johnson in 1852. He and several others stayed on that winter and built the cabin.[5]

5) Parsons King Johnson and Henry Jackson. They conceived the plan to start the townsite, after returning from their riverboat trip in 1850. Johnson and Jackson hired two wood-choppers, Daniel Williams and John James, as well as a teamster, Louis DeMoreau. The five men left St. Paul on January 31, 1852, with Jackson and Johnson leading the way. Three days later, they reached the present-day site of Belle Plaine, where Jackson got sick. He returned to St. Paul while the rest of the party pushed on, arriving at Sibley Mound on February 5.[6]

6) The honor of naming the new town was given to Mrs. Parsons King Johnson (Laura Bivens) and her sister, Mrs. Henry Jackson (Angelina Bivens), the wives of the town fathers.[7] They selected "Mankato," upon the suggestion of Colonel D.A. Robertson, another member of the expedition. Robertson, in turn, had taken the name from the report written by Joseph Nicollet, a French explorer, who had mapped the region in 1838. In it, Nicollet compared the Blue Earth or "Mankato" River with all of its tributaries. Unlike George Featherstonhaugh, a

---

[4]Ken Carley, The Sioux Uprising of 1862, (St. Paul: The Minnesota Historical Society, 1976), 2-3.

[5]Anna Wiecking, As We Once Were: Stories About the Settlement and Life of Blue Earth County From 1850 to the Early 1900's, (Mankato, Minnesota: 1971), 6.

[6]Ulrich, Blue Earth County, 13-14.

[7]J. Fletcher Williams, With an Introduction by Lucile M. Kane, A History of the City of St. Paul to 1875, (St. Paul: Minnesota Historical Society Press, 1983), 484.

British explorer, who had written "Mahkatoh" in his journal from an expedition two years earlier, Nicollet spelled Blue Earth as "Mankato."[8]

7) The name of Blue Earth County's largest city, as well as the seat of its government was derived from the language of the Dakota Indians. "Mahka" or "Manka" means *earth*, "to" means *blue* or *green*. Thus, Mahkato or Mankato translates in English as *Blue Earth*. It was the name given by the Dakota to the largest stream that empties into the Minnesota River near its great bend. The river was so called because of the blue-green clay deposits located along its banks.

The difference in spelling and pronunciation may be due to dialectic differences among different bands of the Santee or Eastern Dakota. Since either form is correct, the fact that "Mankato" was chosen over "Mahkato" as the name for the townsite, suggests that there were other reasons for the selection besides the popular notion that "Mankato" was a misspelling made by bureaucrats in St. Paul when the townsite was chartered. Another popular notion is that when literally translated, "Mankato" means, *blue skunk*.

During the Dakota Conflict of 1862, there was a prominent Dakota warrior chief by the name of "Mankato." He was certainly older than the settlement; therefore he was not named after the town. This fact proves that "Mankato" was an acceptable word in the Dakota language, not simply a mistake in spelling made by government bureaucrats.

8) In historic times, the original inhabitants were the Dakota or "Sioux" Indians. In prehistoric times, it is believed by anthropologists that tribes of Otoe, Omaha and Cheyenne Indians once lived in the Mankato area.

9) Mankato was intended to be built at the confluence of the Blue Earth and Minnesota Rivers. That would have put the center of downtown in Sibley Park.

10) When Johnson and the rest of the party landed, they noticed high water marks on many of the trees, strongly suggesting the presence of spring flooding. They wisely chose to relocate the townsite further downstream, where the great bend of the Minnesota River formed a natural levee or dam that kept the town from flooding.

---

[8]Warren Upham, Minnesota Geographic Names: Their Origin and Historic Significance, (St. Paul: Minnesota Historical Society, 1920, reprint ed., 1969), 61.

11) They called it by its present name, "Minnesota" or "cloudy water."

12) St. Pierre's or St. Peter's River after Pierre Charles LeSueur, who explored the Minnesota River Valley in 1700-1701.

13) St. Paul.

14) They were businessmen. Jackson opened the first store, hotel, post office and justice court in the St. Paul area. It was here, at Jackson's store, that the idea of starting a townsite at the junction of the Minnesota and Blue Earth Rivers was conceived. Johnson, a tailor by trade, was also a member of Minnesota's First Territorial Legislature.[9]

15) Sleighs and cutters. Johnson and Jackson used the frozen Minnesota River as their means of travel because to travel by land, meant cutting their way through dense forests.

16) 1853.

17) It served as the first stagecoach road, linking Mankato to St. Paul and the outside world.

18) The "Mankato House." It was built on the corner of Front and Hickory Streets. Construction was begun in July 1853, by General Samuel Leech. The lumber, millwork and workmen for the building came from St. Paul by boat. Due to ill health, Leech sold the site in 1854 to Henry Shaubut, who completed the construction. A grand ball was held July 4, 1855, to dedicate the hotel.

19) Mankato became the county seat of Blue Earth County, a year after the county was organized in March 1853.[10] Becoming county seat was a major means of ensuring a town's survival on the frontier.

20) The Mankato or Kasota stone quarries. An area, stretching from Kasota in LeSueur County through Mankato and into South Bend Township (Blue Earth County), contained miles and miles of rich dolostone quarry land. [Dolostone is similar in chemical composition to limestone, except that it contains magnesium, instead of calcium. The result is that dolostone is harder and more durable than limestone.] In 1853, George Maxfield started a stone quarry business. Soon others followed,

---

[9]Ulrich, Blue Earth County, 12.

[10]Neill, History of Minnesota Valley, 535.

including: Adam Jefferson, Fowler & Pay, Babcock & Wilcox. Mankato-Kasota Stone and Vetter Stone Company are still in operation as of 2002.

21) The townsite of South Bend was named for the most southerly bend made by the Minnesota River on its entire length. Geographically, South Bend was slightly south of Mankato. Although South Bend held the distinction of being at the river's most southerly point, its greatest shift in direction occurred at Mankato, where the river changed from a southeasterly course to a northeasterly one.

22) St. Peter and Paul's Catholic Parish (1854) and the Presbyterian Congregation. For a short time, the Presbyterians held services in the public school building. They bought a bell which was used for both church and school purposes. The bell was purchased in 1857 with funds raised by the Presbyterian Women. Total cost of the bell was $300.00. It was transported by boat from Cincinnati, Ohio. The bell was used for a variety of purposes—everything from calling children to school to giving the alarm for fires and Indian raids. Many years later, it gave the first news of the end of World War I, on November 11, 1918.[11] Today, (2002) it hangs in the bell tower of the First Presbyterian Church in Mankato.

23) The "Old Log School," built on the site of present-day Union School. Lafayette G.M. Fletcher was the first teacher in the Old Log School. He was paid $35 a month to teach 37 students. Before this school was built, Sarah Jane Hanna and Mary Ann Thompson held private school classes in 1853.

24) The Winnebago, who originally lived in south-central Wisconsin, and spent time on a reservation at Long Prairie, Minnesota, before being relocated to Blue Earth and Waseca counties. Ironically, it was the Winnebago that requested the change. In a rare display of cooperation, Indian officials in Washington allowed the Winnebago to choose their new home where they remained, peacefully, until being forced to move again in the aftermath of the Dakota Conflict. In 1855-56, the Winnebago Agency House was built in McPherson Township. It served as an office and dwelling for the Indian Agent.

25) Postmaster. His leather mail pouch is on display at the Blue Earth County Historical Society in Mankato. In 1854, George H. Marsh

---

[11] History of Century Businesses and Churches, 4 May, 1988.

secured a government contract to pick up the mail every week from Fort Snelling. Before this, the mail arrived infrequently, by river boat. Marsh's first trip was made on foot as far as Traverse des Sioux and by Indian canoe up the Minnesota River. Later, Marsh used two horses and a covered rig to deliver the mail. Within a year, he had increased his mail service to twice a week.

26) Dr. Moses Wickersham was the first-known physician to establish a medical practice in Mankato. He and his brother, Jason F. Wickersham, also opened Mankato's first drug store. Dr. Wickersham was known to bring food as well as medicine to the poor. During the Dakota Conflict of 1862, he provided aid and comfort to the sick and needy.[12]

27) The Enfield Building was built in 1856.[13]

28) It demonstrated to the Dakota Indians the failure of the U.S. Government's attempts to bring the renegade Inkpaduta to justice. "If he can get away with murdering white settlers, then maybe we can too," the reasoning went. This incident set a dangerous precedent that was to have violent consequences when the Dakota took to the warpath against the settlers of the Minnesota River valley in 1862.

29) To provide a cheap source of transportation for supplies and raw materials. There were few roads in the early years; the river served as a vital link between the frontier outposts and the rest of the nation.

30) *Mankato Independent*, first issued on June 13, 1857. It was published by Clinton Hensley and Frank Gunning.

31) Bierbauer Brewery (1857). It was actually the first brewery west of St. Paul. It was operated by Jacob and William Bierbauer.[14]

32) May 11, 1858.

33) The Blue Earth County Fair. The Blue Earth County Agricultural Association held this fair at South Bend. In 1864, the fair was permanently held at Garden City, along the banks of the Watonwan River.

---

[12] Julie Schrader, ed., The Heritage Of Blue Earth County Minnesota, (Dallas: Curtis Media Corporation, 1990), 15.

[13] Ibid., 285.

[14] Ibid., 305.

34) Gottlieb Schmidt. The long-lived family business thrived through several generations and evolved from a harness shop into a retail store. Its inventory featured a wide array of leather goods: luggage, belts, purses and photographic equipment. The company had been part of Mankato's downtown for 127 years, when it closed its doors in 1986.

Bierbauer Brewery (1857). The first brewery west of St. Paul, Minnesota. It was operated by Jacob and William Bierbauer. It was located at the end of Rock Street at North Sixth Street.

The Cummings Ferry operated by the City of Mankato and carried teams, wagons and passengers across the Minnesota River at a point near Sibley Park. This ferry was no longer needed after the first Main Street Bridge was built in 1879.

1860s

1) The first state to offer its troops in defense of the Union during the Civil War was?

2) Minnesota's Governor from 1860-1863, who offered Minnesota's troops to save the Union?

3) Minnesota's first state governor who led militia troops in the Dakota Conflict?

4) The only fort to be attacked in Minnesota during the Dakota Conflict; it was attacked twice.

5) First Blue Earth County soldier to enlist in the Civil War.

6) Public safety institution that was organized in Mankato in 1860.

7) Recruitment center for Mankato's Civil War soldiers.

8) Provided sanctuary for refugees fleeing the Dakota Conflict of 1862.

9) Name of the prison where Dakota warriors were interred awaiting execution.

10) Episcopal Bishop of Minnesota; nicknamed "Straight Tongue" by the Dakota.

11) Responsible for commuting death sentences for many Dakota warriors.

12) The total number of Dakota warriors sentenced to be executed.

13) The number of Dakota warriors actually executed in Mankato on December 26, 1862.

14) Execution of Dakota warriors remains the_____in American history.

15) Pioneer grist mill whose construction was interrupted by the Dakota Conflict.

16) The year the Civil War ended and the School Sisters of Notre Dame arrived in Mankato.

17) The original name for Minnesota State University, founded in 1867-68?

18) What steamship sank in the Minnesota River near Mankato?

19) The process for Mankato achieving its status as a city in 1868?

20) The three communities that formed "Mankato" in 1868.

21) Who was Mankato's first mayor and when was he elected?

22) The device that was used to send messages over a wire.

23) What came to Mankato in 1868? The original tracks ran along Fourth Street.

24) Name the major department store that was founded in Mankato in 1868.

25) The name of the steamboat used to transport surviving Dakota prisoners to Fort Snelling.

26) The name of the Union General sent by Lincoln to assist in putting down the Indian Uprising.

27) Declared in Mankato by the U.S. Army to maintain order during the time the execution of the Dakota warriors was taking place.

28) Given a pardon for turning states' evidence against another prisoner.

29) Hanged by mistake during the execution at Mankato.

30) The name of the doctor involved in removing one of the corpses following the execution. His sons learned anatomy by studying the skeleton of one of the Dakota Warriors.

31) Name of the Dakota leader in the U.S./ Dakota Conflict of 1862.

32) Built on the northern shore of Minnesota Lake in 1864?

33) Purchased by the Mankato Fire Department in 1866.

34) What conveyance helped transport people and goods across the Minnesota River (between Mankato and North Mankato) before the first Main Street bridge was built in 1879?

Answers and Commentary, 1860s

1) Minnesota.

2) Governor Alexander Ramsey was in Washington, D.C. when news reached him that President Lincoln had issued the call for 75,000 troops to "put down the rebellion." This was immediately after the Confederates had fired upon Fort Sumter in Charleston Harbor (April, 1861). Ramsey hurried over to the War Department and pledged Minnesota's support for the Union cause to Secretary of War, Simon Cameron. At the time he did it, Ramsey had no direct authorization. He later telegraphed the news of his actions back to Minnesota, assuring himself that the people of his state would support him. Ramsey was not disappointed.

3) Henry Hastings Sibley. Sibley was a reluctant participant in the Dakota Conflict. He had worked among the Indians for many years as a fur trader, and had many close friends and relatives on the other side. He had an excellent understanding of the Dakota language, customs and culture. It was these qualities that made Sibley the most qualified man to lead a military campaign against the Dakota.

4) Fort Ridgely was originally built in 1853. In contrast to Fort Snelling, Ridgely was poorly constructed. It had no protective wall to guard it from attack. Powder magazines were constructed at the extreme northwest corner of the fort, away from all the other buildings. This made them impossible to defend and practically useless to anyone needing more supplies. Wooded ravines surrounded the fort on three sides, enabling the Dakota attackers to sneak up on their adversaries without being noticed. Had it not been for the presence of artillery, Fort Ridgely would have been forced to surrender, opening the way for the Indians to sweep down the Minnesota River Valley to wipe out all white settlements, including Mankato.

5) James Cannon.

6) Mankato Fire Department. It is one of the oldest organizations in Blue Earth County.

7) Bunker Hill—today it is known as "Highland Park."

8) Mankato House Hotel. There is a story that once the Uprising was over and the refugees had left the hotel, much of the silver was missing! However, this has never been proven conclusively.

9) Camp Lincoln. It was located near present-day Sibley Park. A lynch mob made up of local citizens was turned back one night by soldiers standing guard on the road to the prison. Apparently, these vigilantes were not satisfied to let the government punish the Dakota; they wanted to take matters into their own hands.

10) Henry Whipple of Faribault. He traveled all the way to Washington, D.C. to speak to President Lincoln on behalf of the Indians. Whipple presented his case in six points:
    • Regard the Indians as wards of the state, rather than as sovereign nations.
    • Do not leave the Indians without self-government—leads to "murder and war."
    • Indian Agents must possess high standards of integrity, chosen by merit system.
    • Indian funds must be used to "civilize" Indians, not exploit them.
    • Indian trade practices must be changed to protect Indians, not used to pay debts.
    • Past dealings with Indians have been unfair; that must be corrected.[1]

11) President Lincoln was so moved by Whipple's pleas, he agreed to suspend any planned execution until he could appoint a legal team to review the convictions.

12) Lincoln ordered his associates to list only those who had been charged with murder or rape. He then wrote out the names of the forty men and signed the final order of execution with his own hand.

13) One man died in prison while awaiting execution and one man (Godfrey) was pardoned at the last moment for turning state's evidence against somebody else. In the end, there were 38 Dakota Indians executed at Mankato.

14) Largest mass-execution. The Indians were all executed at the same moment on a wooden gallows specially constructed for the purpose. It consisted of a wooden platform with four trapdoors. Above each trapdoor was a wooden beam on which the nooses had been suspended. Each man was placed with his neck in the noose and his feet on the trapdoor. William Duley, a survivor of the Lake Shetek Massacre cut the

---

[1] Henry Benjamin Whipple, <u>Lights and Shadows of a Long Episcopate: Being Reminiscences and Recollections of the Right Reverend Henry Benjamin Whipple, D.D., L.L. Bishop of Minnesota. With Portrait of the Author and Other Illustrations</u>. (New York: The Macmillan Company, 1889), 139.

central support holding the trapdoors upright. As the four trapdoors swung downward at the same time, the necks of the men in the nooses were broken from the force of the sudden fall. Their weight caused the nooses to pull tight, strangling them.

15) Seppman Mill. It was built between 1862-64 by Louis Seppman and his neighbor, Herman Hegley.

16) 1865.

17) Mankato Normal School. The term "Normal" designated it as a school for the training of teachers. To this day, Minnesota State is noted for its College of Education. Classes were first held in the basement of the Methodist Episcopal Church by Professor George M. Gage. The Normal School building was constructed in 1869 on Fifth Street.[2]

18) On May 10, 1867, the steamship *Julia*, loaded with freight and passengers hit a snag and sank in twelve feet of water near Jefferson Bend. All of the passengers and most of the freight were saved and salvaged. The wrecked hull of the *Julia* remained in the riverbed. Years later, divers recovered the whistle from the *Julia*. It is now in the possession of the Blue Earth County Historical Society in Mankato.

19) Incorporation.

20) Mankato (central downtown area); West Mankato and Mankato City (North Front area from Madison Avenue to north edge of the present city).

21) James Wiswell was elected in 1868 and served as Mankato's first mayor until 1870. He was re-elected in 1875-1879 and again in 1881-1882.[3]

22) Western Telegraph. The first message was received October 21, 1868 by telegraph operator Drake at the Minnesota Valley Railway Depot at Fourth and Van Brunt Streets.

---

[2]The Year of the Sesquicentennial: 150 Years Mankato Area, commemorative timeline, (Taylor Corporation), 2002.

[3]Vernard E. Lundin, At the Bend in the River: An Illustrated History of Mankato and North Mankato, (Chatsworth, California: Windsor Publications, Inc., 1990), 35.

23) The Minnesota Valley Railroad. (Later it was renamed the Chicago, St. Paul, Minneapolis and Omaha or "Omaha" line). The railroad came into the city between Plum and Elm Streets and ran along Fourth Street.[4]

24) Empire Store, later renamed George E. Brett Dry Goods Store.

25) The *Favorite*.

26) John Pope. Pope had been seriously defeated by General Robert E. Lee at the Second Battle of Manasses (Bull Run) in August, 1862. Lincoln sent Pope to the Minnesota frontier after news reached the President that the Dakota Indians were on the warpath. Governor Ramsey demanded that Lincoln send federal troops to assist the local residents. Lincoln refused, claiming that he had no troops to spare. Instead, Lincoln sent Pope as a gesture of goodwill to the people of Minnesota and to get rid of the troublesome general. Contrary to the myth presented by "Dances With Wolves" and other movies, being sent to the frontier was a form of demotion. Pope's inflated sense of his own importance, as a result of this humiliating military assignment, only made a bad situation worse. It was Pope who ordered the Indians to be put on trial, despite Sibley's earlier promises to the Indians that if they surrendered peacefully they would be allowed to go free. The trials hastily convened by Pope's military commission were a travesty of justice, resulting in the conviction and sentencing to death of 303 Indian prisoners.

27) Martial law was declared. No alcohol could be purchased or consumed in Mankato while the execution was taking place. Ironically, years later, the scene of the execution would be depicted on commemorative metal trays distributed by Standard Brewing Company of Mankato. One of their advertising signs also depicted soldiers drinking beer as they watched the execution.

28) Godfrey, a mixed-blood. He was of Dakota and African-American heritage.

29) Chaska, a "farmer Indian". Chaska had saved the life of Sarah Wakefield, the wife of the Upper Sioux Agency's physician. Mrs. Wakefield persuaded Chaska to give himself up to the military authorities at Camp Release, promising that his courage in saving her would keep him safe from harm. He was arrested, imprisoned and "hanged by mistake."[5]

---

[4]Ulrich, Blue Earth County, 40.

[5]Carley, Sioux Uprising, 17.

30) Dr. William Mayo. He received the body of Cut Nose. After years of denial, the Mayo Clinic finally admitted the story was true and assisted in authenticating the skeletal remains and turned the body over to Dakota leaders for burial. Cut Nose was finally laid to rest in traditional Dakota fashion in 1998. Only then, according to Dakota religious beliefs, could his soul finally be at peace.

31) Little Crow. Like Sibley, Little Crow was a reluctant participant in the Conflict; but when his personal honor was challenged by several younger braves, Little Crow knew he had little choice but to lead the assault on white settlements. He eluded capture by escaping into Canada. In the summer of 1863, Little Crow decided to return to his ancestral home in the Minnesota River valley. He was spotted near Hutchinson picking raspberries with his son. Little Crow was shot and killed by farmer Nathan Lamson. For years, the remains of Little Crow were exhibited at the Minnesota Historical Society in St. Paul. Finally, in 1972, Little Crow was laid to rest.

32) Shostag Windmill or the "Haunted Mill." It received its name from the superstitious nature of its builder, Gottlieb Shostag. Shostag had grown up in a community where witchcraft, black magic and superstition were a normal part of daily life. He remained an alien in the American thinking community. He never was able to adapt or assimilate into the technological revolution taking place all around him that brought inventions such as the railroad and roller mill to rural Minnesota. In doing so, these forms of "progress" undermined his business. It became cheaper and more efficient for a farmer to take his grain elsewhere to be ground, rather than bring it to Shostag's mill. Not realizing that impersonal economic forces were at work, it was easier for Shostag to blame his bad luck on the Devil. He became convinced that his mill was bewitched, and that the Devil lived inside, disguised as a black rabbit. One day, Shostag saw the rabbit run outside. There! At last! He had beaten the Devil! No one but Shostag entered the mill after that. He made sure of that by nailing shut all the doors but one. By doing so, Shostag defeated his own original purpose in installing doors all the way around the structure, so that a person would not be decapitated by one of the propellers of the mill when it changed direction to catch the wind. One day Shostag was hit in the head by one of the propeller blades. Pneumonia set in, and Shostag never recovered. It seemed as if his bad luck or paranoia had finally caught up with him. Because of its unique design, isolated location, deteriorating condition from years of neglect following Shostag's death and legends about the black rabbit, Shostag's monument earned the name, "haunted mill." It was destroyed

in 1939, when the dry lake bed caught fire.[6]

33) Its first fire engine. It was a hand-operated pump mounted on a hand-drawn cart. The pump was worked by means of levers and "brakes" (large handles that could be folded up when not in use). It took a dozen or more men to operate the brakes in order to obtain effective water pressure to the nozzle. Water was obtained from cisterns that were located at intervals throughout the town. They had been built for this purpose. This fire engine may still be seen; it is in the collection of the Blue Earth County Historical Society in Mankato.

34) The Cumming's Ferry carried teams, wagons and passengers across the Minnesota River at a point near the present Cedar Haven Lutheran Home, adjacent to Sibley Park, in Mankato. The ferry operated by means of a cable and pulley attached to the opposite bank.[7]

---

[6]Mrs. Charles A. Brecht, "The Old Mill," The Story of Minnesota Lake, (Minnesota Lake, Minnesota: Centennial Committee, 1966), 17.

[7]Mike Lagerquist, ed., The History of North Mankato: Updated in 1998 Upon the City's 100th Anniversary, (North Mankato, Minnesota: City of North Mankato, 1998), 7; Julie Schrader, Heritage of Blue Earth County, 41.

The Seppman Mill (1862-1864) was constructed of native stone and timber found on the Seppman homestead. The mill was impressive in its dimensions. It was thirty feet in diameter at the base, tapering to twenty feet at the top. The mill was 32 feet high to the top of the wall. The dome was another ten feet high, making the structure a total height of 42 feet. At its peak, Seppman's mill could grind as much as 150 bushels of wheat per day.

R.D. Hubbard House
This French Second Empire mansion was built by Rensselaer D. Hubbard in 1871. It was characterized by its mansard roof, covered with polychrome, slate shingles and arched windows. The mansion boasted such luxuries as indoor plumbing (1871), three marble fireplaces, stained glass windows, fabric wall coverings and electrical light fixtures. The house was enlarged in 1888 and was completely redecorated in 1905, the same year that Hubbard died. He was the founder of the Hubbard Milling Company in Mankato.

1870s

1) Created as a "final resting place" in 1870.

2) Townsite platted in 1870; named for twin waterfall called_____ by Dakota?

3) Townsite named for a Winnebago and Dakota Indian Chief; platted in 1871.

4) French Second Empire style mansion, built in 1871.

5) Located at the corner of Main and Fifth Streets; built in 1871.

6) Another name for the "Kern Bridge;" built in 1872 on the Le Sueur River.

7) Began in 1873; lasted four years—destroyed farmers' crops all over Southern Minnesota.

8) Major cash crop of Southern Minnesota during the 1870's.

9) Railroad trestle built in 1874; considered a great engineering feat for it provided an essential means of transporting grain from farmers' fields to processing mills in the Mankato area. Named for a grist mill that was built in 1866, but was destroyed by fire in 1880.

10) Name of Catholic High School; first established in 1875.

11) Passed through Mankato on their way to unsuccessfully rob the Northfield Bank.

12) Built in 1876; potential target of this same gang.

13) Mankato's first bridge; constructed in 1879.

14) Built in 1878; converted to roller process in 1879.

15) Founded by Scottish Immigrants; incorporated in 1878.

16) This decade saw a major achievement in Mankato's public education system.

17) What two diseases were epidemic in 1877?

18) Where was Tinkcomville located, and who was it named after?

First National Bank building. The James/Younger Gang planned to rob this bank, but were thwarted due to the presence of so many people attending the Mankato Trade Fair. The gang chose the Northfield Bank instead. Following the unsuccessful Northfield raid, the fleeing James gang passed back through Mankato.

Answers and Commentary, 1870s

1) Glenwood Cemetery.

2) Minneopa. At one time, the townsite had a hotel, store, blacksmith shop, dance hall, lumberyard, railroad depot and grain elevator.

3) Good Thunder.

4) R.D. Hubbard House. Rensselaer Dean Hubbard was born in 1837 in New York state.[1] He went west to California to seek his fortune. He sold equipment and other supplies to the gold miners in the region; he even tried opening a bank. Discouraged with business opportunities in California, Hubbard planned to return to New York. He decided to take the northerly train route on his way back East, which brought him to Mankato. Hubbard was so impressed with what he saw he decided to settle down and make Mankato his permanent home.

When he purchased the property, there was already a substantial house on the site. Hubbard ordered it removed to make way for the mansion he intended to build. The house was built in French Second Empire architectural style (named for the regime of Napoleon III), because Hubbard wanted to show the world that he was an accomplished businessman. It featured such luxuries as an indoor bathroom, marble fireplaces, stained glass windows and gas lighting (later converted to electricity). Because the city had no means of piping the gas to him, Hubbard built his own gas plant on the grounds in order to operate his light fixtures. Hubbard remodeled his house twice, enlarging it in 1888 and redecorating it in 1905.

Hubbard's first business venture in Mankato was the linseed oil business where he met his future business partner, George Palmer. In 1878, the two formed a partnership and opened a flour mill in downtown Mankato. This was the beginning of the Hubbard Milling Company. Hubbard died in 1905 while away on a business trip to Chicago. He was buried in Glenwood Cemetery in Mankato. The Hubbard House has been owned by the City of Mankato and operated by the Blue Earth County Historical Society since 1938.

5) St. Peter and Paul's Catholic Church.

---

[1]Wiecking, As We Once Were, 23.

6) "Yaeger's" Bridge. It remains the only bridge of its kind (single-span bowstring arch through truss construction) in Minnesota.

7) Grasshopper plague. Schools were closed and trains slid off their tracks from the slippery mass of dead grasshoppers being crushed under their wheels. County Commissioners voted a bounty of ten cents a quart for grasshoppers as an incentive for people to go out and destroy them. So many quarts were brought in that the bounty had to be reduced to five cents a quart because the commissioners feared they would pay out all of the county's funds and bankrupt the county! Later, the state of Minnesota agreed to pay the county back one-half of the sum paid in these bounties. In one ten-day period alone, the County paid out $32,000 for about sixteen bushels of dead grasshoppers.[2]

8) Wheat.

9) Red Jacket.

10) St. Peter and Paul's Catholic School; now Loyola.

11) James-Younger Gang.

12) First National Bank. This building was one of the area's finest examples of Prairie School architecture. The building (later known as the Ellerbe Building) was incorporated into the construction of the Midwest Wireless Civic Center in 1994.[3]

13) Iron truss bridge. The bridge was constructed of three spans of iron beams stretching between hand-laid stone pillars. The span closest to North Mankato was supported in the center by a round pillar that had an iron track on top of it. This feature enabled the span to turn parallel with the river, allowing steamboats to pass. The bridge had a wooden plank floor wide enough for two wagons to pass.[4]

14) Hubbard Milling Company. R.D. Hubbard along with George M. Palmer and William Pearson opened the R.D. Hubbard Milling Company. The mill was one of the largest in southern Minnesota.

15) Mapleton.

---

[2]Ulrich, Blue Earth County, 47.

[3]Mankato Free Press, 15 February, 1989 & special edition, February, 1995.

[4]Schrader, Heritage of Blue Earth County, 258.

16) Nine students graduated from High School in 1876; they were Mankato's first public high school graduating class.[5]

17) Diphtheria and Small Pox.[6]

18) In 1873, James Ray Tinkcom purchased 180 acres in the valley south of Byron Street. He platted the land for 240 residential lots and he built a beautiful tan brick house for his family on the corner of James Avenue and Fairfield Street. Unfortunately, many people believed the area was too secluded and too far away from downtown, schools and the fire station. Only two homes were built in Tinkcomville, Tinkom's and the Joseph Ibach mansion—Chateau De Amour. In Tinkcom's disappointment, he built an eight foot, wrought-iron fence around his property and locked the gate. Finally, in the early 1900's, several families from Syria (now Lebanon) emigrated to Mankato. They settled in Tinkcomville. Others followed and built houses there as well.[7]

---

[5]Ibid., 332.

[6]Wiecking, As We Once Were, 50.

[7]Schrader, Heritage of Blue Earth County, 250, and Blue Earth County Historical Society Newsletter, March/April, 1993.

The Blue Earth County Courthouse was built between 1886-1889 by contractors, Ring and Tobin of Minneapolis. It was constructed of dolostone, obtained from a local quarry. Originally, the building consisted of two full stories, a basement and an attic. A 1965 remodeling project completely gutted the interior. It was remodeled again in 1988, the same year the building was finally formally dedicated.

1880s

1) The most famous of all the "Big Tops" got its start in Mankato on May 8, 1880. What was it?

2) When was Mankato's first telephone line put in operation?

3) When were Mankato's first water mains, gaslines and street lamps installed?

4) When did electricity first come to Mankato?

5) What famous person died in the waiting room of Mankato's Milwaukee train depot, at Fourth and Washington Streets?

6) What famous Mankato landmark was built in 1886-87?

7) Two famous guests that stayed here.

8) When the Blue Earth County Courthouse was built in Mankato, what did not happen?

9) Ran on tracks like a train, but carried passengers around town like a bus.

10) Mankato's largest and best known city park was established in 1887.

11) Original name for the land containing an oval race track, grandstand and whiteboard fence that was also purchased in 1887 and incorporated into the same park.

12) Founded as a medical institution by a former Colonel in the Civil War.

13) Welsh community platted along Minnesota River, northwest of Mankato.

14) Triangular piece of land given to the City of Mankato in the 1880's to be used as a park; site once contained a stately old elm tree and Civil War monument.

15) Billy Mead, local baseball legend, was first pitcher to develop this move in 1889.

16) Used by the "Mankato Baltics" for the first time in 1889.

17) What school was established in 1888 by J.R. Brandrup?

Mankato Baltics Baseball Team (1889)
Pictured in front: L-R – Billy Mead, pitcher and Harry Roberts, catcher. Center: George Peayer, Bill Schellbau, Manager Charley Griebel, Charles Roos and Chuck Wood. Standing: John Dackins, George Frost, George Roos and Albert Roos.

Answers and Commentary, 1880s

1) The Ringling Brothers Circus. It had its first showing on a lot at Second and Cherry Streets, the site of the original YMCA and former GreyHound Bus Depot.[1]

2) 1880. The first telephone line ran from Mankato City Hall to the Hubbard Mill to the Mankato House. R.D. Hubbard was one of the first (if not the first) to have a line connecting his business with his home.

3) 1883. Street lights were lighted each evening and extinguished each morning by a "lamplighter" in Mankato, as early as 1882. Actual distribution of gas to homes and businesses began in 1883. The first wooden water main was installed in 1883.

4) 1885, but it was not until 1910 that service was available throughout most of the town.

5) Schyler Colfax—Vice President of the United States under U.S. Grant; heavily involved in corruption during the Grant administration, including the Credit Mobilier railroad scandal; nicknamed "The Smiler," because he always seemed to be smiling about something; served as Speaker of the U.S. House of Representatives when Lincoln was president. When presiding over the House of Representatives, Colfax spoke so fast, he sounded more like an auctioneer than a speaker. Colfax was Lincoln's first visitor to the White House on the morning of April 14, 1865, arriving while the President was having breakfast. Colfax's mission was to ask Lincoln whether the President was going to call a special session of Congress during the summer. Lincoln's answer was no. Colfax returned later in the day to receive a long message from Lincoln to the miners of the West. Lincoln asked Colfax to attend the theater with him that evening. Colfax declined; he was leaving for California in the morning and wanted to get to bed early. Ironically, Colfax was Lincoln's last visitor on the night he was assassinated. He hurried to Lincoln's deathbed several hours later full of self-accusation at not having been at Lincoln's side when the President needed him most [2]

---

[1] Schrader, Heritage of Blue Earth County, 568.

[2] Dorothy Meserve Kunhardt and Philip B. Kunhardt Jr., Twenty Days: A Narrative in Text and Pictures of the Assassination of Abraham Lincoln and the Twenty Days and Nights that Followed—The Nation in Mourning, The Long Trip Home to Springfield, Foreword by Bruce Catton, (North Hollywood, California: NewCastle Publishing Co., Inc., 1985), 63.

6) Saulpaugh Hotel. It was built by Thomas Saulpaugh. The Saulpaugh Hotel was said to have marked Mankato's transition from a town of wooden buildings and dirt streets to a city of stone and pavement.

7) President William Howard Taft and John Dilinger.

8) It was never formally dedicated until 1988. This was on account of the fact that many Blue Earth County residents believed that building a new courthouse was unnecessary—just another way for Mankato to show off. There was even talk of moving the county seat to Garden City, a more centralized location; that was until the new courthouse was built. Mankato remained the county seat, but old prejudices died hard. There was so much negative feeling generated by the issue that a dedication ceremony wasn't held until just over a century after the courthouse was built.

9) Mankato Street Railway System. The first street car line was laid on Front Street in 1886, and the first street cars were horse-drawn. The business was not profitable, so it was discontinued in 1895. In 1906, the Mankato Electric Traction Company was formed. More street car lines were laid. The new street cars ran in both directions with motors in both ends. They had two wheels at each end, a single-wire trolley, and seated thirty passengers. By 1930, automobiles had created too much competition. As a result, the street cars ceased to exist.

10) Sibley. It was named for Henry Hastings Sibley, who, in 1850, established a trading post near the south base of the large hill (Sibley Mound) on the east bank of the Blue Earth River.[3]

11) Southern Minnesota Stock and Fairgrounds.

12) Tourtellotte Hospital. In 1888, Colonel John Tourtellotte donated $8,800 to the city of Mankato to build a facility to care for the sick. The two-story building, consisting of twenty rooms, was built on Fourth Avenue just outside the northern city limits.[4]

13) Cambria. In Welsh, the name literally translates as "Wales."

14) Lincoln Park.

---

[3]Schrader, Heritage of Blue Earth County, 263.

[4]Lundin, At the Bend in the River, 81.

15) Curveball or 'roundhouse'.

16) Catcher's mask.

17) The Mankato Commercial College. This business school remained in operation until 1979.[5]

Saulpaugh Hotel and Mankato Commercial College. Mankato's most famous hotel was built by Thomas Saulpaugh in 1886-87. It was noted for its luxurious accommodations. Such celebrities as President William Howard Taft, John Dillinger and Al Capone stayed there. The Saulpaugh was torn down as part of Mankato's Urban Renewal Program. The Mankato Commercial College is to the left of the Saulpaugh in the picture.

---
[5]Schrader, Heritage of Blue Earth County, 341.

Mankato's Union Depot. It was dedicated on December 6, 1896. The last passenger train left Mankato on May 23, 1963.

1890s

1) Paper town platted in 1890 by Daniel Morse to be used as a resort community on account of the presence of mineral springs in the vicinity; located in Le Ray Township, Blue Earth County.

2) First cases of this product were sold in Mankato in August, 1890.

3) Built on the corner of Hickory and Fifth Streets in Mankato in 1891.

4) Famous children's author and historical novelist born in Mankato in April, 1892.

5) This author's name for Mankato in her well-known children's stories.

6) What was the Panic of 1893?

7) What service was provided to poor and undernourished children by the Mankato school system?

8) Constructed in 1896, the original building had a clock tower that was later removed when the building was expanded.

9) Built jointly by the Chicago, St. Paul, Minneapolis & Omaha and the Chicago Northwestern lines in 1896—still a landmark in downtown Mankato.

10) Last excursion paddlewheeler to visit Mankato in 1897.

11) When did the first factory-built automobile arrive in Mankato?

12) Built on the corner of Fifth and Washington Streets in 1898-99.

13) Popular sport in Mankato in 1890's and part of a trend sweeping the country.

14) School that opened in 1894 at the request of Mankato residents who were moving from downtown to the hilltop area and closed in 1899.

15) Built in 1898, this Queen Ann style mansion now shelters the YWCA.

16) What was the first funeral parlor in Mankato?

Mankato High School. The Mankato High School was built at a cost of $40,000. It was located at the southwest corner of the intersection of Fifth and Hickory Streets, across from the Blue Earth County Courthouse. It was completely destroyed by fire in 1941, paving the way for the construction of a new high school (Mankato West) ten years later.

Answers and Commentary, 1890s

1) Mankato Springs. In his design for the town, Morse included roads, parks and a gazebo which he constructed. Visitors to the six mineral springs could sit and drink in the health-restoring waters. Morse determined that as much as 35,000 gallons of water flowed daily from the springs. He built a bottling house where the water from the spring was piped in, carbonized and bottled. He also had plans to build a hotel and cottages on the site, but these dreams never materialized. In 1894, Morse sold his "Mankato Mineral Springs Company" to a New York investor, but his plans for development also failed. Morse ended up getting the property back. After failing to find any more interested investors, Morse finally gave up the enterprise in the early 1900s.[1] Morse was ahead of his time; ironically, bottled mineral water is now a lucrative business. What was taken for granted for so long as "free" is now a highly sought after commodity.

2) Bottled mineral water from Mankato Springs.

3) Mankato High School, built at a cost of $40,000. It was located at the southwest corner of the intersection of Fifth and Hickory Streets, across from the Blue Earth County Courthouse.

4) Maud Hart Lovelace. She became the author of six novels and eighteen children's books. She was best known for her beloved series of Betsy-Tacy books, which were a recounting of her childhood in Mankato. Maud Hart Lovelace died in 1980, and was buried in Glenwood Cemetery in Mankato. The Children's Wing of the Blue Earth County Library was named in her honor.

5) Deep Valley.

6) Mankato area banks and others in the nation were ordered to suspend business on August 2, 1893, by telegram from Washington, D.C. Permission to reopen, after examination, was not granted until five weeks later, on September 12, 1893.[2]

7) The school lunch program was established in 1894.

---

[1] Tim Krohn, "Resort Didn't Spring: 19th Century Plans Envisioned a Resort Based on Mineral Springs," The Free Press, (Mankato, Minnesota), fall, 2001.

[2] Mankato Free Press, 18 September, 1993.

8) Mankato Post Office, at the corner of Second and Jackson Streets.

9) Union Depot.

10) *Henrietta.*

11) In 1897, a Stanley Steamer arrived in Mankato by rail. Once unloaded, it was taken out into the street where a crowd had gathered to witness the exciting takeoff. To the amazement of the onlookers, the car reached a terrific speed of six to eight miles per hour! [3]

12) St. Joseph's Hospital.

13) Bicycling.

14) Old East Mankato School. It was closed when enrollment dropped to between 10 and 15 students.

15) Lorin Cray Mansion. It was a two-and-one-half story residence with Classical and Romanesque detailing, designed by local architect, Frank Thayer. Lorin Cray, a prominent judge, lived there with his second wife Lulu. Cray was a native of New York, born there in 1844. He lived in Wisconsin before coming to Blue Earth County in 1859. He served in both the Civil and Dakota Wars. He was admitted to the bar in 1875, and moved to Mankato in 1887. He served as a railroad lawyer, working for both the Chicago, St. Paul, Minneapolis and Omaha and the Chicago/Northwestern Railways. In 1898, Cray was elected Judge of the Sixth Judicial District. Cray was a strong proponent of several civic and religious organizations, particularly the Young Women's Christian Association or YWCA. Cray was instrumental in founding the organization. When he died in 1927, Cray left both his home and a trust fund to the organization. The mansion has been in public use since Cray's death.[4]

16) Lamm and Landkamer built Mankato's first funeral parlor in 1899. It was located at 116 East Main Street. In 1903, a new funeral parlor was built at 116-118 Walnut Street. Later, another funeral home was built at South Second Street.

---

[3] Mankato Free Press, 27 June, 1952.

[4] Schrader, Heritage of Blue Earth County, 26.

U.S. Post Office, Mankato, Minnesota. Built of local dolostone, the Post Office building once featured an impressive clock tower that was removed. The building still stands at the corner of Second and Jackson Streets. The interior lobby area retains much of its original architectural character, such as high, coffered ceilings, brass fixtures, etc.

Mankato Electric Traction Company streetcar. The company was formed in 1906. Construction began in 1907 and the railway began its operations in 1908. Originally, there were two lines of track that were laid. One began at North Broad Street near Tourtellotte Park, ran south on Broad Street to Vine Street, crossed over to Front Street, ran south on Front street to Park Lane and ran on to Sibley Park. The other line began at the corner of Front and Main Streets, ran east on Main Street to Fifth Street, ran South on Fifth Street past the Blue Earth County Courthouse and the Mankato Teachers' College Building (Old Main) to Warren Street, then west to Fourth Street, south to Clark Street, then to Center Street, then to Byron Street, then to Pleasant Street, where it came to an end at the corner of Pleasant and Willard Streets.

1900s

1) Founded in 1900, obtained its product from the Blue Earth River and Spring Lake in January of each year.

2) Built on the site of the former Mankato Linseed Oil Company in 1900.

3) Established in 1901 to preserve and promote the history of Mankato and surrounding communities.

4) Named for its benefactor, Andrew Carnegie.

5) Another name for a "horseless carriage."

6) Dedication ceremonies were held in the large gymnasium of what new building on the corner of Second and Cherry Streets?

7) What business, represented by a red and white pole, was located in the basement of the YMCA building on South Second and Cherry Streets?

8) One of Minnesota's oldest state parks, established in 1905.

9) Name this major North Mankato manufacturing business that began operation in 1905?

10) George Palmer became president of this Mankato company after the death of its founder.

11) First car in the United States to be powered by a V-8 engine.

12) Built at the corner of Washington and Fourth Streets in 1906.

13) Purpose of the Mankato Electric Traction Company, formed in 1906.

14) What was the name of Mankato's first motion picture theater that opened in 1906, on the 400 block of South Front Street?

15) Built at Sibley Park in 1907, this was the beginning of the Sibley Park Zoo.

16) What Mankato street was once called Windmiller Hill?

17) An outbreak of what disease affected more than 6,000 Mankato area people, killed thirty-six and left 500 seriously ill during the summer of 1908?

18) Every New Year's Eve people listened for a sound at midnight. What was this Mankato sound?

19) What significant anniversary did Mankato observe in 1902?

20) Name the U.S. Senator from Mankato who was a close friend of President Lincoln.

Lower Falls, Minneopa State Park. The name "Minneopa" is derived from the language of the Dakota Indians. It means, "water falling twice." Efforts to preserve the falls area resulted in the creation of Minneopa State Park in 1905.

Answers and Commentary, 1900s

1) Mankato Ice Company.

2) Standard Brewing Company located on North Fourth and the southeast corner of Elm Street.

3) Blue Earth County Historical Society.

4) Carnegie Library. The Carnegie Library was constructed in 1902-03 on South Broad Street. A free, public library had been created in 1894 by the Mankato City Council. Books were housed on the second floor of the old YMCA building on South Front Street.

5) Automobile.

6) The YMCA building. After a successful fund drive, a 'modern' facility with a pool, gym and athletic equipment was constructed in 1904. The YMCA was a social hub for young men and boys during the Great Depression and WWII years.

7) The YMCA Barbershop began in 1904 in the front corner of the basement of the new YMCA building. In addition to the hometown trade, the YMCA Barbershop catered to traveling men in town for a few days to sell their wares. After staying the night in one of the YMCA's rooms, traveling men would pay a dime for a towel and shower. Then, they stopped in for a shave. The shop had four chairs and bottles of tonics lined the front of the mirrors. When the YMCA relocated in 1957, the barbershop was moved to a new location above Swenson's Photo Shop on South Front Street. Later, it was moved again; this time to the basement of the J.C. Penney Store. The name of the shop was changed to the Y Barbershop. Bob Klimpel was a barber at the shop for over sixty years.[1]

8) Minneopa State Park. A bill was passed by the State Legislature in 1905, designating 70 acres around the Minneopa Falls to be a State Park.

---

[1] Mankato Free Press, 21 April, 1990.

9) The Mankato Brick and Tile Company, otherwise known as "Stewart Brickyard," was owned by William E. Stewart. Many buildings in Mankato and Blue Earth County were built from brick from Stewart's Brickyard including: the Armory, Landkamer's, Good Counsel Academy, Mankato Citizen's Telephone Company and Hubbard Mill.

10) Hubbard Milling Company.

11) "The Mayer Special." It was built in 1903, in Mankato, by Louis Mayer. The successor to Mayer's blacksmith shop, was Dotson Company, Inc.

12) Immanuel Hospital. Members of the Immanuel Lutheran Congregation purchased the former site of the Omaha Railroad company's roundhouse and turn-table. It cost the church $2,500 to purchase the property. Construction began in 1906 and was completed the same year.

13) To provide Mankato residents with street car service.

14) Majestic Theater.[2]

15) A bear cage.

16) Madison Avenue. A German immigrant named Oswald Windmiller had acquired the land on top of the hill. He raised vegetables and flowers and drove down a narrow, winding ravine (now Madison Avenue hill) in a horse-drawn cart to deliver his produce. His business expanded in the early 1900's with his children, Max, Pauline and Louise Windmiller erecting large greenhouses. This business has remained in the family. Currently, it is known as Hilltop Florists.[3]

17) Typhoid fever. During an unusually hot and humid summer, an outbreak of typhoid fever was found to have been caused by a contaminated city water system. Hospitals were filled to capacity, and St. Peter and Paul's School was turned into a temporary hospital.[4]

18) The Hubbard Mill whistle.

---

[2]Sherry Crawford, ed., Chronicles of A Century: A 100 Year Look at Events that Shaped the History of Blue Earth and Nicollet Counties from 1900-1999. (Mankato, Minnesota: The Free Press, Co., 1999), 28.

[3]Mankato Free Press, 15 February, 1963, & Blue Earth County Historical Society Sesquicentennial Radio Spots, 2002.

[4]Schrader, Heritage of Blue Earth County, 569.

19) Mankato observed its semi-centennial celebration (the 50th anniversary of its founding).

20) Senator Morton S. Wilkinson. Morton S. Wilkinson came to Mankato in 1858. He was elected to the U.S. Senate (1859-1865) and to the U.S. House of Representatives in 1868. It was during his term in the U.S. Senate that he became a close confidential friend of President Lincoln.[5] Despite his friendship with the President, Wilkinson did not share Lincoln's humanitarian views in regard to Native Americans. Along with Congressman William Windom, Senator Wilkinson was instrumental in introducing bills that called for the removal of the Dakota and Winnebago Indians from Minnesota.[6] Wilkinson was well-respected and considered by many to be of a generous nature, but he lacked thrift and died penniless in 1894. During the semi-centennial year in 1902, a granite marker was placed at his gravesite in Glenwood Cemetery in Mankato to honor his memory.[7]

"Mayer Special." The 1903 Mayer 8-cylinder car as it appeared in 1910, after many modifications. It was the first automobile in the United States to be powered by a V-8 engine.

---

[5]Mankato, Its First Fifty Years, 1852-1902. Prepared for the 50th Anniversary of the Settlement of Mankato, (Mankato, Minnesota: Free Press Printing Co., 1903), 156-157, 334-336.

[6]Carley, The Sioux Uprising of 1862, 76.

[7]Mankato, It's First Fifty Years, 156-157, 334-336.

Rapidan Dam was built in 1910 and the first power was generated in 1911. In 2002, the decision was made by Blue Earth County officials to bring in the Army Corps of Engineers to make badly needed repairs. The repair work was completed in April of 2002, but it was only a temporary solution. Blue Earth County Commissioners must decide whether to refurbish the dam completely, build a new one or remove it completely.

1910s

1) This structure, built in 1910, provided Mankato with a source of electrical power, beginning in 1911.

2) The first panoramic photograph taken in Mankato was of the_____, completed in 1911.

3) Mankato's Lutheran College, founded in 1911.

4) Our Lady of _____ Motherhouse and Academy, built in 1911-1912.

5) U.S. President who visited Mankato on October 24, 1911 and spoke at the Opera House.

6) The first summer school classes were held in Mankato's Public School system in what year?

7) May Fletcher was responsible for bringing to Mankato and organizing this youth organization for girls in 1915.

8) Physical education classes for whom began in 1916 in Mankato's Public Schools?

9) Major event in world history, many local young men departed from the Union Depot in Mankato to participate in it.

10) 1918 saw a major outbreak of this disease.

11) Replaced old iron truss bridge across Minnesota River at Main Street in Mankato.

12) What was the title of the novel Sinclair Lewis was writing while living in Mankato?

13) Who was the only Minnesota Governor that hailed from the Mankato-Blue Earth County area?

14) Name this home for children?

15) Who was the Mankato native, who achieved national and international success in the opera world?

16) What was this popular, week-long entertainment event held under a tent?

17) What was the name of the lady whose costume shop outfitted numerous Mankato plays?

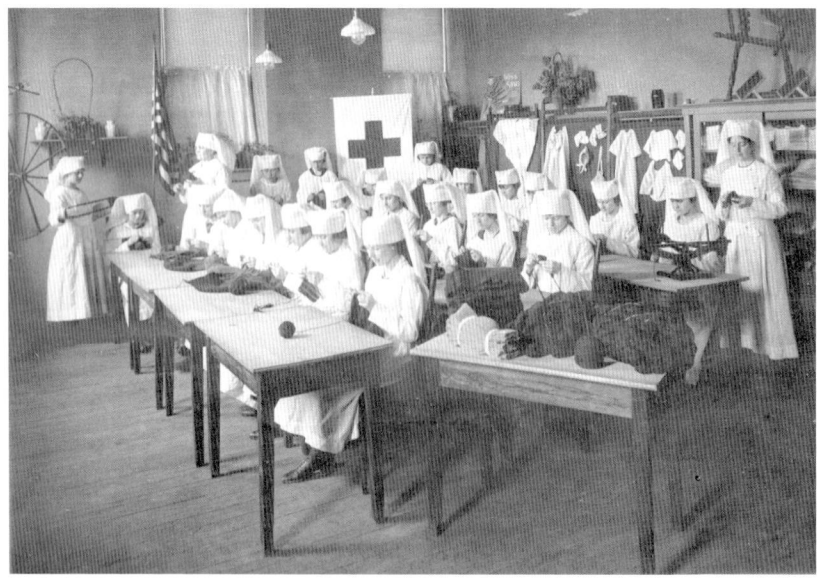

This photograph depicts Junior Red Cross students in class at Mankato High School during World War I. The Red Cross would soon be called upon to fight another war--this time on the homefront. It was the infamous Influenza Outbreak of 1918.

Answers and Commentary, 1910s

1) Rapidan Dam on the Blue Earth River.

2) Red Jacket Bridge. The photograph was taken by local photographer, John Snow. Hundreds of people attended the bridge dedication.

3) Bethany Lutheran College.

4) Good Counsel.

5) William Howard Taft.

6) 1914—the same year World War I broke out in Europe.

7) Camp Fire.

8) Girls.

9) First World War. The United States entered the war in April, 1917; thousands of local men enlisted. Those that remained at home united behind the war effort by buying Liberty Bonds, forming Red Cross chapters, and conserving coal and gasoline needed on the war front.

10) Influenza.

11) The new concrete Main Street Bridge replaced the old iron truss structure. It had ornate light poles that also carried the street car wires.

12) Main Street, published in 1919.

13) Adolph Eberhart. He was elected Lieutenant Governor in 1906 and became Governor of Minnesota upon the death of Governor John A. Johnson in 1909.[1]

14) The Sacred Heart Home for Orphans was established by Father Martin McDonnell and Sister Mary Joseph Crehan and operated from 1909-1915. A two-story home was built on 25 acres of land in West Mankato at the end of Sunset Blvd. Approximately 80 children lived there over the five-year period of operation.[2]

---

[1] Schrader, Heritage of Blue Earth County, 655.

[2] Mankato Free Press, 21 August, 1908 & 25 June, 1910.

15) Florence Macbeth. She became known as 'Minnesota Nightingale' and occasionally came back to Mankato to perform at the Orpheus Club.[3]

16) Chautauqua. This was typically a week-long series of events that featured quality entertainers, orators and scholars. Named for the place of its birth—Chautauqua Lake, New York—the event began as a way to keep frontier settlers enlightened in culture and the issues of the day. Some Chautauquas brought famous people to the Mankato area. In June, 1916, Mankato drew William Jennings Bryan, a famous orator, Democrat and Populist, who made three unsuccessful bids for the presidency. Bryan's arrival was delayed due to a rainstorm, but the crowd eagerly waited several hours to hear him speak.[4]

17) Nora Reedfield. From 1914-1957, she operated a store where she made costumes that were used in many Mankato plays.

---

[3] The Free Press, Mankato, 23 February, 2002.

[4] Mankato Free Press, 20 June, 1994.

Bethany Lutheran College. The Bethany Lutheran College campus has expanded considerably since it was founded in 1911. Its oldest structure, the "Old Main" building still stands on the Bethany campus.

State Normal School. This photograph was taken prior to the 1922 fire that completely destroyed the main building of this institution. A new structure was built on the same site in 1923.

1920s

1) What was the result of the Eighteenth Amendment to the United States Constitution?

2) Legend has it that this famous "bootlegger" and mobster visited Mankato on at least one occasion.

3) Nickname given to Mankato for the presence of covert speakeasies and stills during the 1920s.

4) Nineteenth Amendment to the United States Constitution did what for American women, beginning in 1920?

5) Mankato had its first Winter Carnival in what year?

6) Who built the Ice Palace for the Winter Carnival, and where was it built?

7) What changes were made to Sibley Park in the 1920s?

8) Who was the famous "barnstormer" who in 1921, made a stopover in Madison Lake where his mechanic friend Glen Allyn lived? He also did a show in Mankato.

9) Mankato woman, considered to be the "mother" of the American Legion Auxiliary in the United States.

10) Profession of this Mankato woman.

11) School built in 1921.

12) What was established between Mankato and Minneapolis/St. Paul, beginning in 1923?

13) Fire destroyed the main building of this institution in 1922; a new building was constructed at the same location in 1923.

14) Name this Mankato clothing store that opened in 1924.

15) Eleanor Roosevelt, Guy Lombardo and Sinclair Lewis were several celebrities known to have stayed at this Mankato hotel.

16) What revolutionized show business in Mankato?

17) Mankato Municipal Band was originally known as the _____?

18) Where was Mankato's first airport located?

19) First "troop" organized in Mankato in 1927.

20) Late-night fire destroyed this four-story structure. Thousands of people gathered to watch the blaze.

21) Clara Edwards wrote a song about Mankato. What was the name of this song?

22) Elementary school built in 1928.

23) Boy Scouts first summer campsite from 1928-1947.

24) Average cost of a large glass of beer in Mankato in the 1920's?

25) Cost of a postcard?

26) Cost of a letter?

27) Cost of train fare per mile?

28) Located along Poplar Street was the railroad engine, maintenance and storage building. What was the name of this building?

29) What business did Neil Neilsen purchase in 1921? He expanded it to the point that by 1925 the business encompassed 125,000 square feet and occupied over an entire city block.

Answers and Commentary, 1920s

1) Prohibition of alcohol.

2) Al Capone. There is the story of a young boy from Wells, Minnesota, who came with his uncle to Mankato to buy supplies. No doubt, the boy was fascinated by the hustle and bustle of the "big city." As he was climbing out from his uncle's delivery truck, he noticed a man in a dark suit drop a quarter from his pocket as he was leaving the Saulpaugh Hotel. Apparently, the man didn't even realize he had dropped something from his pocket on to the street because he just kept walking. The boy, forgetting momentarily that he had been warned by his parents to stay close to them at all times and never talk to strangers, grabbed the quarter and ran after the man, calling out, "Hey mister! You dropped this." The man stopped, turned around, and waited for the boy to catch up to him. He smiled as the boy handed him the quarter. The man reached for the coin and took it back but to the astonishment of the youngster, the man put the quarter into his hand. The boy didn't know what to say. He had never been paid so much for so little. The man kept walking and disappeared into the crowd. The boy never spent the quarter the stranger gave him. Later, he saw the man's face again. This time it was in a newspaper. Underneath the photograph was the man's name, "Alphonse Capone."[1]

3) "Little Chicago."

4) Granted them "suffrage" or the right to vote.

5) January 19-24, 1920.

6) The Miller Ice Company cut the ice blocks from the river or lake and hauled them to the Union Depot platform. The Mankato Bricklayer Union No. 11 built the ice palace from the blocks of ice that were cut. The blocks were joined together by a special type of mortar—slush. Once the slush/mortar had frozen, it was just as solid as brick. The palace was used as a backdrop for the royal thrones during the king and queen coronation. The Winter Carnival also featured sled dog races as well as a grand nighttime parade, in which all of the floats and downtown businesses were lit up.[2]

---

[1] Edward M. Stenzel, personal recollection; this was a story the author's father told him as a boy growing up in rural Mankato. Edward Stenzel was born on October 29, 1920. He grew up on a farm in Dunbar Township, Faribault County, during the Prohibition era.

[2] Blue Earth County Historical Society, Sesquicentennial Radio Spot.

7) Additional grounds were added. The grandstand and racetrack with the white fence were torn down. A pavilion was built in 1920. A band shell used to stand near where the parking lots are presently located; it was ruined by vandalism. In May, 1928, the City Council voted to have a driveway to the park built under the Chicago and Northwestern Railroad tracks. This was done to improve safety conditions. Park Superintendent, George E. Blake, had already lost his life at this crossing, becoming the first person to do so.[3]

8) Charles Lindbergh Jr. The location of Lindbergh's show was on Third Avenue, across the road from where the Archer Daniels plant is now located.[4]

9) Helen Hughes Hielscher. She led the campaign to establish the first American Legion Auxiliary in the United States in 1920. By the time she died in 1925, Hielscher saw the Auxiliary become a national organization based on the principles she advocated and promoted.

10) She was a physician, with a lucrative medical practice that she all but gave up to pursue her goal of establishing the Auxiliary. Her husband was Dr. J.A. Hielscher, World War I veteran. Like his wife, J.A. Hielscher was a prominent member of many Civic and Veterans' organizations.[5] In honor of Dr. Helen Hughes Hielscher's role in founding the national American Legion Auxiliary movement, the lower hall of the Mankato American Legion Post 11 has been designated "Hielscher Hall" in her honor.

11) Lincoln School, built on the site of the old Pleasant Grove School on the corner of Pleasant and Byron Streets.

12) The first bus line.

13) Mankato Normal School.

14) Matt J. Graif and partner, Bill Marso, opened the Matt J. Graif clothing store in 1924, at 310 South Front Street. In 1930, they moved the business to Walnut and Front Streets. In 1962, Matt J. Graif and his son John, purchased the National Citizens Bank building on Front and

---

[3]Schrader, Heritage of Blue Earth County, 264.

[4]Ibid., 568.

[5]Ibid., 346.

Hickory. They moved their store to this location in 1963. The store has remained in the Graif family and continues in operation in 2002.[6]

15) The Ben Pay Hotel. In 1925, a six-story building was erected beside the original hotel building, increasing its capacity to 200 rooms. The hotel was owned and operated by the sons of Benjamin, Frank and W.H. Pay. The hotel was closed in 1963, and the building was torn down in 1967.[7]

16) In 1927, "talking pictures" came to Mankato.[8]

17) Mankato Elk's Band.

18) In 1928, Mankato's first airport was near what is now Minnesota State University, Mankato.[9]

19) Boy Scouts of America. The first troop to organize in Mankato was Troop 3, sponsored by the Veterans of Foreign Wars. Although this troop has since been dissolved, three more troops came into being in Mankato in 1927. The new Minnesota Valley Area Boy Scout Council grew rapidly. Three months after its inception, there were 13 troops with a total membership of 227 scouts. By December 31, 1927, membership had grown to 477 scouts in 24 troops. A year later, there were 36 troops with a membership of 851 scouts. By December, 1929, 50 troops had been organized with 1,000 boys enrolled in the scouting program. Of the 50 troops in the council, eight of them were in the cities of Mankato and North Mankato: Troop 3, sponsored by the VFW; Troop 4, sponsored by the American Legion; Troop 12, sponsored by the Centenary Methodist Church; Troop 17, sponsored by Franklin School; Troop 18, sponsored by the Episcopal Church; Troop 24, sponsored by the Knights of Columbus; Troop 28, sponsored by Roosevelt School and Troop 29, sponsored by the North Mankato Public School.[10]

20) St. Peter and Paul's Catholic School. There were 800 students enrolled at the time. The community offered great support to the parishioners by providing classroom space so classes could continue while a new school was being built at Sixth and Main Streets. It was at this time that the

---

[6]Mankato Free Press, 17 June, 1995.

[7]Schrader, Heritage of Blue Earth County, 279.

[8]Ibid., 261.

[9]Crawford, Chronicles of a Century, 56.

[10]Schrader, Heritage of Blue Earth County, 348.

decision was made to separate the students into two buildings. K-8 students attended the St. Peter and Paul's grade school while a new building (Loyola) was built on Fifth Street to house grades 9-12 (boys only). It was not until 1934 that girls were admitted to Loyola.

21) "By the Bend of the River." It was copyrighted in 1927.

22) Franklin School. The new building, designed for junior high students, was built on the site of the Old Franklin School, built in 1874-75. At one time or another, students of elementary, junior high and even senior high ages have attended Franklin.

23) Camp Patterson.

24) Five cents. It was served with two slices of bread with a large helping of roast beef, or a bun with a wiener and sauerkraut on it. (This menu was featured at the Frank Mettler Bar in Mankato.)

25) One cent.

26) One and one-half cents.

27) Three cents per mile.[11]

28) The Omaha Railroad Roundhouse. Construction for a new Roundhouse was begun in October 1929, to replace the old roundhouse at the same location that had been damaged by a tornado in June. The new Roundhouse provided room for eight engines, compared to only four stalls in the previous structure.[12]

29) Neilsen Florists. Neil Neilsen purchased the greenhouses established in 1875 by Herman Lorenz and located on the corner of State and Marshall Streets. By 1925 Neilsen had increased the greenhouses to 125,000 square feet of glass. After Neilsen's death in 1941, the floral complex was operated by his descendants until 1968 after which the property was sold. In 2002 the property was occupied by a gas station, The Lutes building, Dairy Queen West and an apartment complex.[13]

---

[12]Ibid., 571.

[13]Mankato Free Press, 25 October, 1929.

[13]Schrader, Heritage of Blue Earth County, 298

Mankato Winter Carnival Parade, 1920.

The 100 Block of South Front Street. Automobiles (left to right): 1930 Chrysler, 1925 Model T Ford, 1926 Pontiac and 1925 Essex.

1930s

1) What was the name of an early Mankato drive-in restaurant near Sibley Park?

2) Name the building on South Second Street which featured entertainment for area residents for many years that was torn down in 1931?

3) Moved in 1931 from its original location in Mankato Township to stand at the site of Henry Sibley's trading post in Sibley Park.

4) What "first" did North Mankato receive in the 1930's?

5) Depression agency responsible for enabling many students to attend college.

6) Prohibited in college dorm rooms during this time.

7) Means of transportation for most college students during the 1930's.

8) A puppy that was acquired to comfort a lonesome lion at the Sibley Park Zoo.

9) This famous pair became Sibley Park Zoo's most widely-publicized attraction in 1932.

10) Both animals received so much attention that they were exhibited as part of _____ in 1934.

11) Responsible for the death of the Sibley Park Superintendent in November, 1934.

12) This was drilled in Sibley Park in 1935.

13) Built on the Blue Earth River at Sibley Park as a Works Progress Administration project in 1935.

14) What other WPA projects were implemented in the Mankato area in 1935?

15) On June 23, 1936, Briney Gorman of Nashville, Tennessee, described this Mankato park as "hard to beat" for its excellent tourist campsites. This was no small praise, for Gorman was an accomplished tourist camper, having traveled through twenty-five states in two years.

16) Harvey Anderson opened this winter business in 1937, to take advantage of two of Mankato's natural resources—hills and snow!

17) What was Mankato's first radio station that began broadcasting in 1938?

18) The coming of what highway gave hope for improved intrastate transportation?

Mutt and Jeff., the inseparable couple from Sibley Park Zoo.

Answers and Commentary, 1930s

1) The Oasis Drive-Inn. Clyde Wykoff opened it in 1931. It was located on a wedge-shaped lot on Park Lane, just two blocks from Sibley Park. The specialty was hot roast beef sandwiches served on rye bread that sold for ten cents, nickel hot dogs and root beer. Wykoff had a music stand built on top of the building. Every night, from eight to eleven o'clock and Sunday afternoons, a three-piece orchestra would play on the roof. In 1943, the drive-in had used up its entire sugar allotment used to make root beer. As a result, the drive-in was forced to close seven weeks early. The Oasis had several owners over the years. The last of the owners was Al Bell. The drive-in closed in 1975.[1]

2) The Mankato Opera House was built in 1882. It was the center of culture and popular entertainment in Mankato. Many famous stars of the time appeared on its stage including: Mary Pickford, Anna Held, John Drew, Irish tenor, Chauncy W. Olcott and John Philip Sousa's Band. The Opera House also featured Mankato's own Andrews Opera Company, Florence MacBeth and Lora Lulsdorff.[2]

3) Ott Cabin. Originally, George Ott came to Blue Earth County from Indiana in 1857. The cabin was built in Mankato Township, about four miles east of Mankato. The idea to preserve the cabin was that of C.A. Nachbar. He persuaded the Blue Earth County Historical Society to relocate and renovate the cabin. With the cooperation of city officials, the project was successfully completed.

4) North Mankato received its first police car.

5) National Youth Administration or N.Y.A.

6) No one was allowed to smoke or have radios in the dorm rooms. Each dormitory had a dorm "mother" to ensure that all the rules were being followed. There were those who violated these rules, of course. Dorm rooms were strictly segregated. Few girls got to see boys, unless one was coming over for a date. In such instances, the boy had to wait in the "escort room" while the "bell girl" rang the proper room. An "escort slip" had to be signed, indicating name of date, time leaving and time returning.

---

[1] Restaurant Magazine, May, 1946 and Mankato Free Press, 6 December, 1975.

[2] Blue Earth County Historical Society Newsletter, October 1980-January 1981.

7) They walked wherever they went. The only students who could afford to drive were the Mankato students who had access to the family car.

8) The puppy's name was "Jeff." The lion's name was "Mutt." The two grew up together and became inseparable.

9) "Mutt" and "Jeff."

10) The Chicago World's Fair.

11) A black bear, the superintendent had raised from a cub, mauled him to death.

12) The first city well.

13) A Kasota stone dam that created a nineteen acre lake. It was removed following the 1951 flood because the presence of the dam was blamed for a loss of fishing, along with increased pollution that made the water unfit for swimming and the tragic loss of the Mayor's son, who was drowned while swimming near the dam.

14) The Tourtellotte pool and bathhouse, stone stairways and park buildings (including the grand picnic shelter) at Minneopa State Park and several city, water and sewer projects.[3]

15) Highland Park.

16) Skihaven (now Mount Kato).

17) KYSM AM.

18) Highway 169.[4]

---

[3] The Year of the Sesquicentennial: 150 Years Mankato Area. commemorative timeline, (Taylor Corporation), 2002, and Julie Schrader, Heritage of Blue Earth County, 264.

[4] City of Mankato, Community Calendar, 1984.

Oasis Drive-Inn. Clyde Wykoff opened this popular restaurant in 1931. Its specialty was hot roast beef sandwiches served on rye bread that sold for ten cents, nickel hot dogs and root beer. It was located on a wedge-shaped lot on Park Lane, just two blocks from Sibley Park.

President Harry Truman speaking in Mankato, 1948. Both President Truman and his rival, George Dewey, visited Mankato while making "whistle stop" tours across the country, as part of the Presidential election campaign of 1948. Truman logged over 31,000 miles and spoke to about 6,000,000 people. His speeches were described as being "homely, down-to- earth, hard-hitting talks," aimed at the common man. Note the microphone President Truman was speaking from. It was labeled with the call letters "KYSM." It remains Mankato's oldest radio station, broadcasting for the first time in 1938—ten years before Truman and Dewey squared off.

1940s

1) Destroyed by fire on July 14, 1941.

2) The first step to bringing this factory to Mankato began in 1940 by Mayor Frank J. Mahowald. Because it would be located in the most important canning section of the entire country, the Mankato plant was expected to be one of the parent company's most important units. Work was begun on the plant on August 16, 1941; it was in production by April, 1942.

3) Two local men, killed in the Japanese attack on Pearl Harbor on December 7, 1941.

4) A local rationing board was created in January,1942, to oversee the rationing of what products during WWII?

5) What caused the Mankato business economy to slow down significantly, during the early stages of WWII?

6) The death of one of Sibley Park's dynamic duo in 1942 left the other inconsolable.

7) Type of trip hammers manufactured by the Mayer Brothers (Dotson Company) firm in the 1940s. Used by the U.S. Army and Navy for emergency maintenance on their bases during WW II. The quality of these hammers was so superior to any of the competitors on the market, the Army and Navy set up a quality specification named for them.

8) What was the name of a popular entertainment center, built in 1945, on Chestnut Street in Mankato?

9) What institution was approved as the first area vocational school in Minnesota?

10) Which two presidential candidates visited Mankato as part of the Presidential election of 1948?

11) What well-known business started as a letter service in the basement of a North Mankato resident in 1948?

12) What was the name of this local group who performed live at noon on KYSM radio during the 1940s?

13) What metal was to be turned in to the local grocer during World War II?

14) Many of the Civil War and World War I cannons displayed in Mankato parks disappeared in the 1940s? Why was this?

15) Highway 22, from Mankato to Mapleton, had commemorative trees planted as a tribute to Blue Earth County's servicemen and women. What was the name given to this road?

16) What epidemic from the 1940s closed Mankato theaters?

Answers and Commentary, 1940s

1) Mankato High School. Classes were held at Lincoln School for the next ten years. The fire began the day summer school students picked up their report cards. As devastating as the fire was, it could have been much worse if classes had been in session. As it was, it took all available firemen 29 hours to finally bring the fire under control; there were rumors of arson that have never been fully dispelled. At the time, there were those that claimed to have heard a loud explosion just before the building burst into flames. Investigators later concluded that the "explosion" sound heard was caused by the force of the flames as they raced through the building's ventilation system and reached the structure's metal roof.

2) Continental Can Company.

3) Vincent Eberhart and Quentin Gifford. Eberhart, 22, son of Mrs. Clara Eberhart, was stationed on the battleship Arizona when it was struck by Japanese bombs. Quentin Gifford, 20, son of Mr. and Mrs. Frank Gifford, was killed aboard the battleship Oklahoma during the initial attack.[1]

4) New cars, inner tubes and other commodities such as coffee, sugar, meat and canned goods.

5) Building permits in Mankato dropped 80 percent.[2]

6) "Mutt," the lion, died in 1942, leaving "Jeff," the dog, inconsolable.

7) "Little Giant." The standard was, "Little Giant or better!"

8) The Kato Ballroom (currently known as the Kato Entertainment Center). The ballroom's early days began as a 1935 fixture of the Blue Earth County Fairgrounds. Built at its current location in 1945, it was host to many swing and polka bands. However, fire destroyed this building in 1953, and the existing ballroom was rebuilt in 1954. Many famous performers such as Louis Armstrong, Count Basie, Glenn Miller, Guy Lombardo, the Beach Boys, Jerry Lee Lewis and countless local performers have played at the Kato Ballroom.[3]

---

[1]Schrader, Heritage of Blue Earth County, 14.

[2]Tim Krohn, "Tragedies Mark Time: Mankato's History is Also Defined by Sour Moments in History," The Free Press, (Mankato, Minnesota), 26 January 2002.

[3]Website, MSU Reporter (Betsy Alwin) and Mankato Free Press, 2 September, 1995.

9) Mankato Area Vocational Technical Institute.

10) Harry Truman and Thomas Dewey. Harry Truman arrived at the Union Depot on October 12th and made an early morning speech from the rear of the presidential special train. A group of 8-10,000 people gathered to hear him speak. The next day, Dewey arrived and spoke to a large crowd.[4]

11) William Carlson established "Carlson Letter Service" in the basement of his North Mankato home. It became Carlson Craft in 1974.

12) The Sunshine Boys. KYSM had developed a noontime program sponsored by the Hubbard Milling Company's livestock feed division. The Sunshine Boys were: Curtis "Swede" Johnson, Maurice Piche, "Spike" Haskel and Gene "Peewee" LaFond. The group became the studio orchestra whenever background music was needed at the station. They were known as the "Jolly Millers," when they played for dances. After World War II, the radio Sunshine Boys became a trio composed of Swede Johnson, Maurice Piche and Paul "Lefty" Alexander. Their theme song was "You are my (Hubbard) Sunshine."[5]

13) Tin. Mankato was designated as a regional shipping point for the statewide collection of tin. The *Mankato Free Press* reported that housewives must realize that it was their patriotic duty to clean and deliver used tin cans to the grocery store in their neighborhood for regional collection. It was estimated that if every household participated in the tin can collection, Minnesota alone would yield 2,100 tons of salvaged tin cans per month, just from household use.[6]

14) They were melted down for scrap metal during WWII.

15) Victory Highway. In the early 1940s, Mrs. Paul Barney organized and coordinated the Victory Highway tree-planting project. It was not completed until 1952.[7]

16) Polio.

---

[4]Schrader, Heritage of Blue Earth County, 372.

[5]Mankato Free Press, 28 July, 1983.

[6]Mankato Free Press, 20 October, 1942.

[7]Blue Earth County Historical Society Newsletter, November, 1985.

Mahowald's Sporting Goods & Hardware, ca. 1940s. Frank J. Mahowald started the Mankato Cycle Company at 624 North Front Street in 1911, with a complete stock of bicycles and motorcycles. In 1916 he expanded the store to include an entire line of hardware and sporting goods.

The Flood of 1951. This view is looking south. The Main Street Bridge is at the center, Mankato is to the left and North Mankato is to the right of the picture. Note: The heaviest flooding was on the North Mankato side of the Minnesota River. There was no natural levee to protect the downtown area as there was on the Mankato side. The flood was caused by an unusually heavy snowfall the previous winter, followed by a rapid warm-up. Because the ground underneath the snow was still frozen, the meltwater had no place to soak in. Instead, it ran off into the rivers, causing them to overflow their banks.

1950s

1) What organization was founded in 1950 by a group of local musicians?

2) Moved from the Kost Garage to a new, separate building at 51 Park Lane.

3) Construction on this building was delayed due to World War II and disputes over where it should be built; it finally opened in 1951.

4) Hundreds of acres of land in Mankato and North Mankato were inundated; many residents were forced to flee their homes in the night.

5) Responsible for the deaths of Claude Bengston and five other local men in the 1950s.

6) What did Mankato celebrate in 1952?

7) First men's dormitory built in 1952.

8) What grocery store was built on Park Lane in 1953?

9) What was the name of a band that took its name from a local dairy?

10) Name changed in 1957 from Mankato Teachers' College to?

11) Opened on the upper campus in 1959.

12) Name of women's dormitory, opened in 1959.

13) Name given to the expansion of the college campus, beginning in the 1950s.

14) What popular singers were killed in a plane crash, shortly after performing at the Kato Ballroom in Mankato, in 1959?

15) The early Mankato streetcar barns on North Broad Street became a church. What is the name of this church?

The 200 block of South Front Street (Walnut Street intersects), ca. 1950. The Grand Theatre is featuring "Stars and Stripes Forever." Other businesses are Tillisch Optometric Eye Parlor, Club Royal, Boston Shoe Repairing, Patterson L. Mercantile Co., Stephenson Music Co., Minnesota Valley Natural Gas Co., Ulrich's Home Appliances, Schmidt's Leather Store, Singer Sewing Machine, Nyquist Clothing Co. and Queen Frock's.

Answers and Commentary, 1950s

1) Mankato Symphony Orchestra. Dianne Pope has been the conductor of the Mankato Symphony Orchestra since 1983.[1]

2) The Mankato Area Vocational-Technical Institute.

3) Mankato High School (now Mankato West). In 1945 with the end of World War II, Mankato residents were ready to consider building a new high school. Several proposed sites were discussed: the old Fifth Street site, Hilltop athletic field, Hilltop location at Main and Division (for a time, this seemed the likely choice) and the Memorial Field site (called the "slough" by its detractors). In the beginning, the School Board unanimously rejected the Memorial Field site, and the selection process remained controversial for four years until finally, the Memorial Field or "slough" site was chosen. The new high school was far enough along in its construction in order for graduation ceremonies to be held there in the spring of 1951. Even severe flooding in April, which inundated the 20-acre school plot with water from the Minnesota River, did not dampen the spirit of the graduating seniors. The school officially opened in the fall of 1951, with 690 students enrolled. In 1959, the east wing of the school was added.

4) The Flood of 1951; known to many local residents as "The Great Flood." There have been other floods in the history of Mankato and North Mankato, both before and since (1881,1908,1965,1993,1997). However, this one held a special place in the psyche of the people. Hundreds of acres of land in both towns were covered by the flood waters, but that was only part of the reason. The waters rose up so quickly due to rapid spring thawing and after an unusually heavy snowfall the previous winter, that many residents had to flee their homes in the middle of the night—adding to the surprise, confusion and sense of fear many people experienced. North Mankato bore the brunt of the river's wrath. It is lower in elevation than its sister city, Mankato. The bend of the Minnesota River formed a natural levee on the Mankato side that kept the town from flooding as easily as North Mankato.

5) The Korean War; sometimes referred to as, "the Forgotten War."

6) The centennial of its settlement.

7) Searing Hall.

---

[1] Lundin, At the Bend in the River, 72.

8) Madsen's Super Valu. Earl Madsen started his business with a grocery store on South Front Street in 1946. In 1953, he built Madsen's Super Valu on Park Lane (now Riverfront Drive). In 1963, he doubled the size of the store. In addition to groceries, the expansion included: hardware, a pharmacy, clothing and other general merchandise—one stop shopping with everything under one roof. Eventually, Madsen would open other stores in Mankato (Madison East), Waseca, New Ulm, Fairmont and Bloomington. In 1976 the business was sold to Randall Stores Inc., a Mitchell, South Dakota based firm. However, the name was not changed to Randall's until 1985. In March, 2001, the roof collapsed from heavy snow, and the building was razed. It was replaced by Cub Foods the same year.[2]

9) The Marigold Dixielanders Band brought lively marching-style Dixieland to thousands of parades and festivals in the Midwest. It started in 1956 as a novelty band in an American Legion parade. Three of the men worked at the Marigold Dairy, so the group put on milkmen's coveralls and visor caps as a marching band uniform. The original Dixielanders were: Lowell Schreyer, Dave "Doc" Evans, Jim Hayes, Gary Claridge, Len Ryan, Terry Powell, Ron Steinberg, and Ellie Stemig. Musicians continued to weave in and out of the Dixielanders and in 1961 the band broke up. It reorganized with Schreyer, Steinberg, Harry Neisen and Jerry "Rip" Kirby to form Michaels' Minstrels.[3]

10) Mankato State College.

11) Wilson Campus School. It was the forerunner to many of the charter school and alternative school programs available at the dawn of the twenty-first century. The school was nationally recognized for its innovative teaching methods based on student choice and self-directed learning through individualized and small group discussion. The school was forced to close its doors in 1978, due to declining enrollment and budget cutting measures undertaken by University President, Douglas R. Moore.

12) Crawford Center.

13) Upper Campus Expansion.

---

[2] Mankato Free Press, 4 January, 1989 & 10 March, 2001.

[3] Mankato FreePress, 12 April, 1984.

14) Buddy Holly, Ritchie Valens and J.P. Richardson, 'The Big Bopper,' played at the Kato's 1959 Winter Dance Party, just days before their plane crashed near Clear Lake, Iowa, on February 3, 1959.[4]

15) Our Savior's Lutheran Church.

---

[4]Website, MSU Reporter (Betsy Alwin) and Mankato Free Press, 2 September, 1995.

Front Street in the 1960s. This photograph was taken during the Christmas season and it depicts an unobstructed Front Street, prior to the construction of the new public library, Holiday Inn Hotel and Mankato Mall in the 1970s and 1980s.

1960s

1) What school was built on the site of an old brewery?

2) This major highway was re-routed in 1960-61 to the western edge of Mankato, taking traffic off of Mankato's Front Street business district.

3) Name of Mankato's television station which began broadcasting in 1960.

4) Longest running program on this station; first broadcast in 1961.

5) What was the name of this traveling truck that Mankato children so eagerly awaited?

6) A vaccine for what disease was given in mass quantities in Mankato, in 1962?

7) Tidal wave of three million gallons of soybean oil from a ruptured tank at this Mankato processing plant was responsible for an environmental disaster along the Minnesota and Mississippi River watersheds in January, 1963.

8) This disaster prompted the creation of this state agency.

9) Assassination of this President in Dallas, Texas, caused many local residents to cluster around their radios to hear the latest news. As in so many other communities across the country, Mankato residents never forgot where they were or what they were doing when the tragic news first reached them.

10) Two brothers, Robert "Bob" Frederick and Marcel "Sal" Frederick built their first restaurant in 1963. Name this restaurant.

11) What was the name of the first major development on Madison Avenue?

12) Reason for the visit by Vice President, Hubert Humphrey and Governor Karl Rolvaag in 1965. Altogether, sixty-two businesses were damaged and 1,600 Mankato residents were forced to evacuate, as a result of this natural disaster.

13) Name the four members of the Mankato rock group called "The Gestures," at the time it received national fame for the hit song, "Run, Run, Run."

14) Caused severe damage to the Hubbard Flour Mill in 1966. The mill was rebuilt.

15) A landmark business in Mankato since 1856, and a survivor of Prohibition was forced to close in August, 1968.

16) George Stoltzman was the first local man to be killed in this War, which led to widespread student protests on the Mankato State College campus.

17) Upper campus buildings that were constructed during the 1960s.

18) Beginning in 1966 Mankato State College became the summer home of this team.

19) This mall opened in 1968 on Mankato's hilltop.

20) These two hospitals consolidated to form in 1968?

21) Supermarkets began to replace neighborhood grocers. What did the supermarkets offer to be exchanged for catalog merchandise or cash to lure customers?

22) Who was Mankato's "Mr. Softee" between 1929 and 1967?

23) What was the name of Mankato's only spy movie produced in 1965 by the Mankato Rotary Club?

Answers and Commentary, 1960s

1) Jefferson Elementary School was built in 1960-61 on the old Ibach Brewery property. The caves in the hillside were once used for storage for the brewery.[1]

2) Highway 169.

3) KEYC., Channel 12 (CBS) The call letters reflected a popular slogan at the time; Mankato was regarded as the "key city," due to its geographic location in the heart of south-central Minnesota as well as its historic status as the retail hub of southern Minnesota and northern Iowa.

4) Bandwagon. Originally it was sponsored by John Deere.

5) The Mister Softee Ice Cream truck. Mister Softee first appeared in Mankato in 1960. Many children (author included!) have fond memories of the chime of the Mr. Softee truck coming down their street in the summertime.[2]

6) Polio. Clinics were set up in schools and other public buildings in Mankato on December 3, 1962, to dispense the new polio vaccine. The largest number of doses (4,000) were issued at the Saulpaugh Hotel at the rate of 1,000 per hour. An estimated 9,350 people were given a dose of type 1 Sabin Polio vaccine by noon the first day.[3]

7) Honeymead Products.

8) Minnesota Pollution Control Agency.

9) John F. Kennedy.

10) Happy Chef. This was the first of fifty-six Happy Chef Restaurants in seven states.[4]

The author remembers his parents taking him there as a boy. Besides the fun of "making the chef talk," by pushing the button underneath; there were the special, little cakes given to young children to celebrate their

---

[1] Schrader, Heritage of Blue Earth County, 330-31.

[2] Mankato Free Press, 22 August, 1994.

[3] Mankato Free Press, 3 December, 1962.

[4] The Free Press, Mankato, 23 February, 2002.

birthdays. A special postcard was mailed in advance to each child, reminding them to ask for their complimentary birthday cake. The author remembered eagerly anticipating the arrival of this card (addressed to the child) in the mail.

The Madison Avenue Happy Chef Restaurant served its last meal on Thursday, April 4, 2002. It was decided to close this store and tear it down, along with Ruttle's 50s Grill, to make room for a new Walgreen's store.

11) Eastgate Shopping Mall was opened in 1964. The building housed a drug and variety store, Lewis Eastgate Drug and Mueller's Superway (grocery). Later that same year, the Hilltop Shopping Center opened with a Gamble-Skogmo discount store, "Tempo," as its first tenant. This mall later became the Belle Mar Mall.[5] Tempo was eventually replaced with a "Red Owl" grocery store, a Red Owl "Country Store," and "Marketown Foods." The site is currently occupied (2002) by RiverBend Academy Charter School.

12) The Flood of 1965. In addition to the politicians, Mankato was being patrolled by the Minnesota National Guard while city workers reinforced dikes built with 900,000 sandbags. Sixty-two businesses in Mankato were damaged. 1,600 residents were evacuated. Sibley Park suffered so much damage from the flooding that it was decided to permanently remove the herd of bison (buffalo) from its zoo. These animals were relocated to Blue Mounds State Park near Luverne, Minnesota, where their descendents can still be seen.

13) Bruce Waterson, Gus Dewey, Tom Klugherz and Dale Menton.[6]

14) An explosion and fire.

15) Mankato Brewing Company.[7]

16) The Vietnam War.

17) McElroy Center (1961); Highland Arena and Blakeslee Stadium (1963); Gage Center A (1965); Gage Center B (1967); Armstrong Hall,

---

[5]Crawford, <u>Chronicles of a Century</u>, 70.

[6]<u>Mankato Free Press</u>, 31 July , 1996.

[7]Krohn, "Tragedies Mark Time," <u>Free Press</u>, 26 January, 2002.

Performing Arts Center and Memorial Library were ready for student use (1967); Morris Hall finished (1968). Groundbreaking for the Centennial Student Union was held in 1967, the centennial of the legislation creating Mankato Normal School. For years, the MSU seal featured 1867 as the founding date; it was changed to 1868 to reflect the actual opening of the Normal School in that year. Mankato Normal School was Minnesota's second institution of this type. Only Winona had a Normal School older than Mankato's.[8]

18) The Minnesota Vikings.

19) Madison East.

20) Immanuel (125 beds) and St. Joseph's Hospitals (236 beds) combined in November, 1968 to form Immanuel-St. Joseph's Hospital.

21) Gold Bond or Green Stamps.[9]

The author remembers his mother and older sister pasting stamps into these coupon books so they could order an item that would become somebody's Christmas present, birthday present, etc. The fun part was to look through the premiums catalog, but pasting the stamps was a tedious chore for which the author, as a young boy, had little patience.

22) James "Tony" Golias. He came to Mankato from Greece and operated a horse drawn popcorn wagon at the corner of Front and Jackson Streets. Golias was a friend of Lee Fischer, owner of Fischer's Clothing Store. Although he would occasionally move his business to some other location, the Fischer Clothing corner was Tony's favorite spot. He used an "old country" concoction which was referred to as "bear grease." It wasn't exactly butter, but whatever it was, "bear grease" was a big hit with Tony's youthful fans. The money he earned selling popcorn in Mankato sustained both Tony and his family back in Greece. In 1967 Tony returned to Greece at age 87.[10]

23) Man on a Mission. It was filmed on location in Mankato and featured many local landmarks including: the Union Depot, Schmidt House (former YMCA), Seppman Mill and more. Local citizens were recruited as actors and actresses.

---

[8]Schrader, Heritage of Blue Earth County, 344.

[9]Mankato Free Press, 29 March, 1989.

[10]Ken E. Berg, 'Tony' R.I.P., Mankato Free Press, 7 March 1973.

Mankato City Bus. These orange and white buses, owned and operated by Mankato City Lines, were once a common sight in Mankato. They were eventually phased out of existence when the City of Mankato created its Mass Transit system in 1975.

Edward M. Stenzel retired from driving Mankato's city buses on November 1, 1985, after twenty-six years of dedicated public service to the citizens of Mankato/North Mankato.

1970s

1) In 1970, what facility was relocated six miles north of Mankato in Lime Township, Blue Earth County?

2) The first one of these was held in 1972 to "honor" the thirty-eight Dakota warriors executed in Mankato. It has become a major cultural event held every September, near the confluence of the Minnesota and Blue Earth Rivers.

3) Who was responsible for bringing the World Plowing Contest to Blue Earth County in 1972?

4) Construction of this facility in 1973 split the Mankato High School into two campuses.

5) This hit Mankato area on January 10, 1975, paralyzing the region for several days.

6) The City of Mankato took over operation of this service, beginning in 1975.

7) Name of Mankato State College changed to what in 1975?

8) A forerunner of Mankato's Urban Renewal campaign, this building was built in 1976. It was built across Front Street, paving the way for the eventual construction of an indoor shopping mall along what had once been Mankato's busiest commercial street.

9) This event was first held on the Robert Schroeder farm in Lincoln Township, Blue Earth County, to commemorate the Bicentennial of the American Declaration of Independence in 1976. Despite torrential rains and horrendous mud, the event was successful enough to become an annual festival of agriculture.

10) Construction of this began in 1977-78.

11) The older portion of this church building (originally built in 1924) burned in April, 1978.

12) What Mankato school graduated its last class in 1978?

13) Mankato's premiere "Marching Ambassadors" organized in the late 1970s.

14) After several years of duel usage, these two merged in 1979.

Photograph taken at the dedication of the Minnesota Valley Regional Library's Maud Hart Lovelace Wing, May 21, 1977. L to R: Kelley Reuter, Caroline Nicholas (granddaughter of Marion Everett, character of Carney in the Betsy-Tacy books), Merian Lovelace Kirchner (daughter of Maud Hart Lovelace) and Shirley Lieske (Children's Librarian). Kelley Reuter and Caroline Nicholas were the co-chairmen of the Lovelace Library Wing committee.

Answers and Commentary, 1970s

1) Mankato Airport. Jets prompted the need for a new municipal airport with longer runways. The new airport facility was opened in 1970.[1]

2) Powwow or "wacipi."

3) Bert Hanson. The World Plowing contest was held on 1,400 acres of land near Vernon Center, owned by fourteen farmers. Hanson donated his entire farm for the event. More than 500,000 people attended the seven day event.[2]

4) Mankato East.

5) A huge blizzard. On Friday, January 10, 1975, the National Weather Service was predicting a strong storm. It started snowing Friday morning and by that afternoon the visibility was near zero. Winds were gusting up to 60 mph. By Saturday, the storm was being compared to the Armistice Day Blizzard of 1940. Tragically, fourteen people lost their lives during that blizzard, nicknamed "the storm of the century."[3]

As a seven year old boy, the author remembered playing on the floor in the living room of his parent's home, when the lights suddenly went out. Since it was early evening, there was a long time to wait in the dark before it was bedtime. Bryce's mother, Arlene Stenzel, lit a kerosene lamp that was kept for just such an emergency. Fortunately, the kitchen stove was natural gas operated and the oven kept the house relatively warm and comfortable while the blizzard raged outside. However, at one point, Bryce remembered his parents having to bundle themselves up to go outside to check the gas regulator that was threatening to freeze up. The gas company refused to send out a service person into the whipping winds and blinding snow, but they did offer some advice over the phone. Armed with kettles of boiling water, Arlene and Edward (Bryce's father) disappeared into the snow and made their way to the regulator. They poured the water over it to thaw the line. Bryce's older sister, Laurie, and he watched anxiously from the kitchen window, but could see very little in the whirling snow. They had been given strict instructions to stay inside. While they were outside, Edward and Arlene also tended to their poultry and other livestock. After what seemed years to Bryce, they finally returned to the safety of the house. The storm raged

---

[1]Crawford, <u>Chronicles of a Century</u>, 83-84.

[2]ibid., 76.

[3]Blue Earth County Historical Society, Sesquicentennial Radio Spot.

all night. The wind sounded as if it was trying to tear the roof off the house. But once the gas line crisis was past, it was kind of fun to be snowed in. It took several days for the streets and roads to be cleared. The snow drifts were so high people literally had to dig out of their houses. Paths were like tunnels through the snow. Although other blizzards have come and gone since then, the blizzard of 1975 set the standard as far as Bryce Stenzel was concerned.

6) Mass Transit.

   Bryce Stenzel remembered his father taking him on a drive to see the new bus routes that he (Bryce's father, Edward Stenzel) soon would be driving. The routes were so new there were still burlap bags covering the route signs. Bryce's father had driven the orange and white city busses belonging to the firm of Ed and Donald Wold for many years. Now the City of Mankato was taking over ownership of the bus line. In addition to the new routes, there were new buses as well.

7) Mankato State University.

8) Minnesota Valley Regional Library (now Blue Earth County Library). The Saulpaugh Hotel was also a victim of the Urban Renewal craze. It was torn down in the 1970s, and was eventually replaced by the Holiday Inn.

9) Farmfest '76.

   Bryce's father (Edward Stenzel) drove one of the shuttle buses from Mankato out to the site, bringing spectators to the event. Bryce remembered only two things about what was touted as a 'once in a lifetime event,' slipping and sliding as he tried to walk around the grounds with his mother and the filthy condition of the bus after the mud from the people's feet was tracked all over.

10) Mankato Mall.

11) Bethlehem Lutheran Church, at the corner of Second and Liberty Streets.

   Bryce remembered arriving at school and hearing that the church he and his family attended was on fire. His teacher had her radio on as she was preparing for that day's lesson. That evening, Bryce and a friend walked from the YWCA building down to the church to survey the damage. From the outside, the church seemed to be intact, but they could see that the large front balcony window had been completely broken out. Black smudges were all around the edges of the window, testifying to the intense heat and smoke that had been within. For months after the fire, the entire Sunday School wing of the building smelled of charred wood and smoke. Even after the rooms were repainted, the odors from the fire remained.

12) Wilson Campus School. MSU's innovative Wilson Campus School graduated its last and largest class of eighty-eight seniors in May 1978, closing its doors, despite local protests.[4]

13) Mankato Area 77 Lancers Marching Band. Mark Sivanich, Community Services Director and Edwin Stock, Musical Director were instrumental in organizing the band. The Lancers are currently (2002) under the direction of Tedd Gullickson, Director of Bands at Mankato West High School.

   Bryce's sister, Laurie Stenzel, was a member of the Lancer's First Edition. Later, Bryce himself would be a member of the group from 1983-1986.

14) Highland and Valley Campuses of Mankato State University.

---
[4]Mankato Free Press, 26 May, 1978.

Photo of Thomas Miller (sculptor) and Amos Owen (Dakota Spiritual Leader) at the June 1988 Dedication Ceremony for the "Winter Warrior". Thomas Miller was responsible for carving several memorials out of native Mankato dolostone . Two of his works are the "Winter Warrior" (1988) and the "Buffalo" (1997). Amos Owen was instrumental in establishing the "Mahkato Wacipi" and other efforts aimed at raising public awareness about injustices committed against Native American inhabitants (Dakota) of the area by white settlers. The most notable of these was the hanging of the thirty-eight Dakota warriors in 1862. His collaboration with Thomas Miller resulted in two new memorials being erected near the site of the execution. Owen was also instrumental in the creation of "Reconciliation Park."

1980s

1) When Mankato's Lincoln Elm tree was cut down in 1980, its growth rings were counted. How old was the tree determined to be?

2) This college began classes in Mankato, beginning in 1983.

3) What building was built in 1886 and razed on October 23, 1985?

4) What 80-year old building was razed in 1984 to make way for the new Veterans' Memorial Bridge?

5) Replaced Main Street Bridge across Minnesota River in 1985-86. It was designed to compliment the U. S. Army Corps of Engineer's Flood Control Program by being built high enough to go over the floodwall instead of through it. It was also designed to allow rail traffic to pass under it. Motorists were no longer forced to stop and wait for trains, as in the past.

6) 1987 was proclaimed as_____ in order to commemorate the 125th anniversary of the Dakota Conflict.

7) Mankato sculptor responsible for carving the "Winter Warrior" statue in 1987, commemorating the execution of the 38 Dakota warriors. He would later design other memorials in the Mankato area: Vietnam Veterans', Korean, World War II and the Buffalo in Reconciliation Park.

8) What historic building was reincarnated as a retirement home?

9) This institution moved its headquarters from the R.D. Hubbard House to the upper floor of the old Newman Center building in 1988. This paved the way for the restoration of the Hubbard House to its former Victorian elegance.

10) Name this popular tourist attraction on Mankato's Broad Street and North Mankato's Mary Circle?

11) What three things resulted in the Great Farm Depression affecting Blue Earth County and Midwest farmers?

12) When did Mankato break the record for highest temperature?

13) This structure was completed on the MSU campus in 1989. It symbolized the past, present and future of the institution.

14) Gus-Johnson Plaza was named for a prominent Mankato attorney and was converted from what building?

Answers and Commentary, 1980s

1) The Lincoln Elm tree was determined to be 315 years old.[1]

2) Rasmussen Business College.

3) The Odd Fellows Building. "The city wanted the building demolished to make a flashier entrance for the Mankato Mall."[2] The slab of Mankato stone, bearing the symbols of the Order of Odd Fellows (a linked chain with crowns), is currently propped against the side of the Carriage House, adjacent to the R.D. Hubbard House in Mankato. It is all that remains of the imposing building.

4) The Burton Hotel. This Mankato landmark was built in 1905. Edward Himmelman opened his new hotel, the Hotel Heinrich, on June 2, 1905. The grand new hotel had wide staircases, spacious halls and comfortable rooms. Guests dined in the Palm Room which featured Kasota stone pillars as well as a mosaic tile floor. In 1936, the hotel was sold to W.G.A. Burton. The name was changed to the Burton Hotel.[3]

5) Veterans' Memorial Bridge.

6) The Year of Reconciliation.

7) Thomas Miller.

8) Old Main. Old Main was built in 1924 after fire destroyed the Mankato Normal School in 1922. The building was abandoned in 1979 when Mankato State moved to its upper campus location. In 1988, Old Main was renovated into the Old Main Village Retirement Community.[4]

9) Blue Earth County Historical Society.

10) Celebration of Lights. During the Christmas season, spectacular light and decoration displays became a tradition in these neighborhoods. Tour busses brought people from all over to view these displays.[5]

---

[1]Schrader, Heritage of Blue Earth County, 263.

[2]Mankato Free Press, 31 December, 1985.

[3]Mankato Free Press, 31 May, 1993.

[4]Mankato Free Press, 30 June, 1988.

[5]Lundin, At the Bend in the River, 95.

11) High land prices, low crop prices, and double-digit interest rates.[6]

12) July 31, 1988. In 1988, area temperatures registered 100° F on June 19th and 20th. Northern States Power records showed an all time peak energy usage. July ended with Mankato's hottest day in fifty years—a record 107°. It was the sixteenth day in July registering over 90°.[7]

13) The Alumni Plaza and Ostrander Bell Tower. The stone arch for the plaza was taken from the historic Old Main Annex, symbolizing the University's rich history.[8]

14) Immanuel Hospital.[9] The older section of the hospital was torn down to make room for the newer portion of the Gus Johnson complex. However, the newer wing of the hospital was incorporated into the design of the new senior retirement facility.

It was in this wing (then part of Immanuel Hospital) that the author was born on March 27, 1967.

---

[6]Crawford, Chronicles of a Century, 96.

[7]Mankato Free Press, 29 December, 1989.

[8]The Year of the Sesquicentennial: 150 Years Mankato Area, commemorative timeline, Taylor Corporation, 2002.

[9]Schrader, Heritage of Blue Earth County, 293.

Immanuel Hospital was built on the corner of Washington and Fourth Streets in 1906. This building was converted into Gus Johnson Apartments.

Mankato City Hall. Once the home to many of Mankato's city offices, this building was torn down in 1996 to provide additional parking space for surrounding businesses.

1990s

1) Built in 1990 to provide interpretive services for school children and visitors to Rasmussen Park in Mankato.

2) Mankato's new Middle School, named by students in honor of the region's Dakota Indian heritage. It was built in 1991.

3) Mankato's largest shopping mall was built in 1991. It further expanded growth of retail and industry to Mankato's east side.

4) Name Mankato's first Bed and Breakfast.

5) Freak storm on October 31, 1991.

6) This Mankato retail landmark closed its doors in 1992 after 124 years of business in the community.

7) Built in 1993-94, it boasted a 7,300-seat arena, enabling Mankato and the surrounding area access to big-name entertainment previously available only by commuting to the Twin Cities.

8) Credited with saving Mankato from massive damage from the Minnesota River when it reached its highest level in recorded history after torrential spring rains.

9) What public building was located on Jackson Street, across from the Post Office?

10) Built in Sibley Park in 1994, it replaced a similar structure from the 1920s.

11) Responsible for the death of John Janavaras, a fifteen year old Mankato boy, and the hospitalization of nine other people. One of the largest mass vaccinations took place in the aftermath, with about 30,000 residents between the ages of 7-29 receiving shots at the rate of almost 800 per hour.

12) What was caused by a faulty air-conditioning unit on the roof of the Mankato hospital? It was responsible for the death of one man and the sickening of 16 others.

13) Name this county trail that was once the abandoned Milwaukee Road railbed.

14) What was dedicated in September, 1997?

15) This tore through both Comfrey and St. Peter on March 29, 1998, causing severe damage.

16) Local artist, Marian Anderson, created a series of three Mankato historical collages and North Mankato's centennial painting. What were the titles of these paintings?

17) Agencies housed in the new Mankato Intergovernmental Center, built in 1998.

18) Mankato State University changed its name to this in 1998?

19) After being drained in the 1920s, this lake was restored in 1998-99.

20) Construction began on this new Southern Highway Route connecting what two highways?

Answers and Commentary, 1990s

1) The Mankato Elk's Nature Center at Rasmussen Woods Park. Laurie H. Stenzel (sister of the author) was the first Naturalist at Rasmussen Woods. She was responsible for the creation of the Rasmussen Woods Environmental Education Program, beginning in 1987.

2) Dakota Meadows.

3) River Hills Mall.

4) The Butler House, located at 704 South Broad Street. The house was built in 1905 by Mortimer Currier, a wealthy candy-maker and mayor of Mankato, from 1899-1901. Charles Butler purchased the house in 1923. In 1929, he sold it to Frank Clements. Several years later, Clement's granddaughter married Charles Butler Jr. The house was given to the couple as a wedding gift. In April, 1992, Nancy Willette and John Seitzer purchased the house from the Charles Butler estate and opened it as a Bed and Breakfast. Owners in 2002 are Ron and Sharalyn Tschida.[1]

5) "Halloween Blizzard".

6) Brett's Department Store.

7) Mankato Civic Center (Midwest Wireless Civic Center).

8) Massive concrete floodwalls.

9) Mankato City Hall. The building was originally built in 1927, as the regional headquarters for the Standard Oil Company. The City of Mankato purchased the building in 1956, where it had its offices for many years before relocating to the new Intergovernmental Center.[2]

10) The Leas Schwickert Arts Pavilion.

11) Meningitis outbreak.

12) Legionnaires' Disease.

---

[1] Mankato Free Press, 11 July, 1992.

[2] Mankato Free Press, 21 November, 1994.

13) The Red Jacket Trail was opened in 1997.[3]

14) Reconciliation Park. It was established through the cooperation of the Mankato-Dakota communities on the site of the 1862 execution.

15) F3 level tornado.

16) Partners In Progress-1994
    Closing Time-1995
    Good Ol' Summertime-1996
    Yesteryear-1998

17) City of Mankato and Mankato Area Public Schools offices.

18) Minnesota State University, Mankato.

19) Indian Lake, which had been a farmer's field for eight decades, was restored as an open-water lake.[4]

20) Officially named Blue Earth County Road 90, the new highway opened in 1999, and connected Highways 169 and 22.[5]

---

[3]Julie A. Schrader, History of the Red Jacket Valley, (Mankato, Minnesota: Minnesota Heritage Publishing, 2001), 57.

[4]Ibid., 69.

[5]Ibid., 53.

Mankato Area 77 Lancers Marching Band at North Mankato Fun Days Parade, July 11, 1998. The Lancers Marching Band is composed of students in grades 9-12 from all the Mankato High Schools: East, West, Loyola and Immanuel Lutheran. Since 1979, the Lancers have delighted audiences throughout the United States and Canada with their precision marching style and stirring music. They have won top honors in numerous parades, band competitions, and fieldshows. The Lancers have been nicknamed, "Mankato's Marching Ambassadors."

Mankato Civic Center. An integral part of Mankato's downtown revitalization was the construction of the Mankato Civic Center (Midwest Wireless Civic Center) in 1993-94. It boasts a 7,300-seat arena, numerous conference rooms and a wide variety of entertainment options. Note the Ellerbe Building (First National Bank) to the left side of the photograph. It was incorporated into the design for the new Civic Center complex to preserve its distinctive architectural features.

2000-2002

1) Businessman, Glen Taylor was responsible for contributing money for the construction of which two structures in Mankato/North Mankato?

2) What was Mankato's first, independent, charter school opened in September, 2000?

3) In the aftermath of September 11, 2001, who came to the Midwest Wireless Civic Center to speak on bioterrorism? He spoke on the evening of November 14, 2001 to a packed house.

4) How many years old will Mankato be on February 5, 2002?

5) Well-known Mankato City Council woman died in February, 2002; known as the "conscience of Mankato."

6) What was the population of Mankato in 2002, the Year of the Sesquicentennial?"

7) What will the future hold for Mankato and its people?

Winter Carnival in front of the Midwest Wireless Civic Center in Mankato. The Carnival was revived to celebrate the Sesquicentennial of Mankato's founding and settlement. It was held February 8-10, 2002. Sleigh rides were advertised, but a lack of snow forced sleighs to use wheels. The Intergovernmental Center is in the background.

Answers and Commentary, 2000-02

1) Taylor Athletic Center, located on the Minnesota State University campus and Taylor Library in North Mankato.

2) RiverBend Academy. In its first year, 150 students were enrolled. When school opened in the fall of 2001, enrollment had increased to 164 students. RiverBend's Mission Statement proclaimed:

   "RiverBend Academy will provide a purposeful place to empower every student to succeed in their school, in their community and in their life."

3) Dr. Michael Osterholm, Director of the Center for Infectious Diseases at the University of Minnesota. He was the State Epidemiologist during the 1995 meningitis outbreak in Mankato. He described the way in which Mankato residents responded to the crisis as being a role model for the rest of the nation.

4) 150 years. The Mankato Midwest Wireless Civic Center hosted its first annual Winter Carnival event to kick off 'The Year of the Sesquicentennial' in 2002. It was held on February 8, 9 & 10.

5) Arline Brown served on the City Council from 1969-1989.

6) Mankato's population in 2002 was 31,477. The combined population of Mankato and North Mankato was 44,200 in 2002. In 1950, the census recorded 18,711 people. Mankato had gained 12,706 people since the year of its centennial 1952. When Mankato celebrated its fiftieth anniversary in 1902, the population was only 16, 080.[1]

7) Only time will tell!

---

[1] Mankato City Directories: 1902, 1950, City of Mankato website 2002 www.ci.mankato.mn.us

Veterans' Memorial Bridge. It was built in 1986 by the U.S. Army Corps of Engineers as part of their flood control program. This bridge replaced the old Main Street Bridge across the Minnesota River. The bridge was also designed in such a way as to allow trains to pass underneath it, without motorists having to wait for the trains to move before they could cross the bridge.

Appendix

Winter at Minneopa Falls.
1999

The Lorene with its barge, the O.K. Dubuque was used as an excursion riverboat on the Minnesota River near Mankato from 1908-1911. Technically, the Lorene was the last riverboat to ply the waters of the Minnesota River; not the Henrietta.

Minnesota River Steamboats, 1850-1897

1850: Anthony Wayne; Nominee; Yankee.

1851: Benjamin Franklin, No. 1; Excelsior; Uncle Toby.

1852: Black Hawk; Enterprise; Jenny Lind; Tiger.

1853: Black Hawk; Clarion; Greek Slave; Humboldt; Iola; Shenandoah; Tiger; West Newton.

1854: Black Hawk; Globe; Greek Slave; Humboldt; Iola; Minnesota Belle; Montello; War Eagle.

1855: Berlin; Black Hawk; Equator; Globe; H.S. Allen; Humboldt; J.B. Gordon No. 2; Montello; Reveille; Shenandoah; Time and Tide.

1856: Berlin; Clarion; Equator; Globe; H.S. Allen; H.T. Yeatman; Humboldt; Minnesota; Reveille; Time and Tide; Wave.

1857: Antelope; Clarion; Equator; Fire Canoe; Frank Steele; Isaac Shelby; J. Bissel; Jeannette Roberts; Medora; Minnesota; Ocean Wave; Red Wing; Time and Tide.

1858: Antelope; Belfast; Clarion; Equator; Fire Canoe; Frank Steele; Freighter; Isaac Shelby; Jeannette Roberts; Medora; Minneopa (barge); Minnesota; Ocean Wave; Time and Tide.

1859: Antelope; Belfast; Favorite; Frank Steele; Freighter; Isaac Shelby; Jeannette Roberts; Minneopa (barge); Ocean Wave; Time and Tide.

1860: Albany; Antelope; Eolian; Favorite; Frank Steele; Jeannette Roberts; Little Dorrit; Minneopa (barge); Time and Tide; Victor (barge).

1861: Albany; Antelope; Eolian; Fanny Harris: Favorite; Frank Steele; Jeannette Roberts; Victor (barge).

1862: Albany; Antelope; Ariel; Clara Hines; Favorite; G.H. Wilson; Jeannette Roberts; New Ulm Bell; Pomeroy.

1863: Albany; Antelope; Ariel; Eolian; Favorite; Flora; G.H. Gray; Jeannette Roberts; Pomeroy; Stella Whipple.

1864: Albany; Ariel; Express; Firesides; Henderson (barge); Jeannette Roberts; Mollie Mohler; Monitor; St. Cloud; Stella Whipple; Turtle.

1865: Addie Johnson; Albany; Annie Johnson; Ariel; Chippewa Falls; Clara Hines; Enterprise; G.H. Gray; G.H. Weeks; General Sheridan; Julia; Hudson; Lansing; Mankato; Mollie Mohler; Otter; Stella Whipple; Tiger.

1866: Addie Johnson; Albany; Alice; Ariel; Chippewa Falls; Damsel; Delaware; Enterprise; Flora; G.B. Knapp; G.H. Gray; G.H. Weeks; G.H. Wilson; General Sheridan; Hudson; Jenny Baldwin; Julia; Lady Pike; Lansing; Mankato; Minnesota; Mollie Mohler; Otter; Pearl; Pioneer; Plant (barge); Stella Whipple; Tiber.

1867: Ariel; Chippewa Falls; Clipper; Ellen Hardy; Flora; G.B. Knapp; Hudson; Jeannette Roberts; Julia; Mankato; Mollie Mohler; Otter; St. Anthony Falls; Tiber.

1868: Ariel; Ben Campbell; Buckeye; Chippewa Falls; Clipper; Cutter; Ellen Hardy; Flora; G.H. Wilson; Hudson; Jeannette Roberts; Mankato; Otter; Pioneer; Wyman X.

1869: Chippewa Falls; Ellen Hardy; Jeannette Roberts; Mankato; Otter; Pioneer; St. Anthony Falls; Tiger; Wyman X.

1870: Dexter; G.B. Knapp; Jeannette Roberts; Mankato; Otter; Pioneer; St. Anthony Falls; Tiger.

1871: Hudson; Mankato; Otter; Pioneer.

1872: Osceola—one trip.

1873: Osceola—two trips.

1874: Osceola—one trip.

1876: Ida Fulton; Wyman X.

1886: Alvira—one trip.

1897: Henrietta—one trip.[1]

---

[1] Thomas Hughes, "Steamboating on the Minnesota River," <u>Minnesota Historical Society Collections</u>, 10, part 1: 158-160.

The Henrietta. This was the last commercial steamboat to dock in Mankato. It made its one and only trip on April 21, 1897. It was a stern wheel vessel, 170 feet long with 40 staterooms.

Coming to Terms With the Past: The Dakota Conflict of 1862

The execution of the thirty-eight Dakota warriors at Mankato, on December 26, 1862, remains the largest mass-execution in American history. Not surprisingly, there have been a wide range of strong opinions and emotional expressions, both on how the event should be remembered, as well as how the location of the execution site should be marked. Immediately after the event, those who wrote the histories of the Conflict described the Indians, who were involved, as "blood-thirsty savages." Consequently, they deserved punishment for "massacring" innocent, white settlers on the frontier. Little attention was given to the underlying causes of the war, such as treaty violations by the government agents sent to protect the Indians, or encroachment by settlers on Indian lands. More recently, efforts have been made to tell the story from the Native American perspective to the point that earlier efforts to commemorate the struggle have been ridiculed and discarded.

The most notable of these attempts to revise history in favor of the Dakota side involved the removal and banishment of the original granite marker that was erected in 1912. On its surface was inscribed in raised letters: "HERE WERE HANGED 38 SIOUX INDIANS, DECEMBER 26, 1862." Critics of the monument argued that the memorial should be removed because it gave no details about the hanging or the events that led up to it. Even worse, the revisionists claimed the marker was blatantly racist, on account of the fact that the word "Sioux" was used (a nickname originally given to this group of Indians by French explorers who had borrowed it from the Ojibway Indians they first encountered. The Dakota (Sioux) and Ojibway (Chippewa) had been bitter enemies centuries before the French explorers came to Minnesota. Not surprisingly, the Ojibway called their enemies by an insulting name. Translated, the name meant, "snake").

Those that advocated removal of the memorial marker won the battle. The stone marker, weighing several tons, was taken down and put into storage. In 1987, as part of the "Year of Reconciliation," a new plaque was erected by the Minnesota Historical Society, detailing the background of the U.S.-Dakota War, the hanging at Mankato and its aftermath. Two new memorials were erected to the memory of the Dakota warriors, the Winter Warrior and the Buffalo. In September 1997, Reconciliation Park was established.

Despite these efforts, there were those determined to destroy the old marker as a way to vent their rage and frustration against past discrimination toward

Native Americans. Over the years numerous threats have been made to throw the marker into the river, grind it up to be used as road fill, pour red paint all over it, etc. Such attitudes have forced less militant individuals to "hide" the marker as a means to keep it from being destroyed. Their purpose in doing so was to ensure that if, at some future date, some agency or organization decided to give the marker a place to be properly displayed as a representation of another time and point of view, they would be able to do so.

It should be pointed out that, contrary to popular belief, those who erected the marker in 1912 (the fiftieth anniversary of the hanging) did not intend to insult or humiliate Native Americans. In his dedication address, Judge Lorin Cray (himself, a Civil War veteran) admitted there had been some opposition to the erection of the monument at Front and Main Streets, and that he could not refrain from answering the criticism. Cray said, "This marker was not so placed to flaunt before the public that we hanged the Indians. It was erected in an entirely different spirit, to perpetuate the immediate history of the region, permitting handing down the history to the generations to come in a correct manner." Editor John C. Wise, of the *Mankato Daily Review*, echoed this same sentiment when he remarked that he had no patience for those that indulged in criticism of the marker. He argued that every stranger who landed in Mankato asked to see the location of the hanging. Even President William Howard Taft did so when he visited Mankato. In Wise's view, the monument marked a site and carried neither praise nor blame.[1]

Anna Wiecking, author of: As We Once Were: Stories about the Settlement and Life of Blue Earth County from 1850 to the Early 1900's, summed it up when she said, "Historians, officials of historical societies and other citizens take the view that the monument marks a very important national historic event, and that we need to profit from history, not try to reject or cover it up."[2] Only when the charade of hiding the marker from short-sighted destruction has ended and it is allowed to be displayed in its proper historical context, along with proper explanation regarding its controversial inscription will the citizens of Mankato truly come to terms with their past. In doing so, Native Americans and whites will finally reconcile their differences.

---

[1] Wiecking, As We Once Were, 46.

[2] Ibid., 45.

Bibliography

Berg, Ken E. 'Tony,' R.I.P. <u>Mankato Free Press</u> (Mankato, Minnesota). 7 March 1973.

Blue Earth County Historical Society Newsletter. October 1980-January 1981.

Blue Earth County Historical Society Newsletter. March/April, 1993.

Blue Earth County Historical Society Newsletter. November, 1985.

Blue Earth County Historical Society Sesquicentennial Radio Spots, 2002.

Brecht, Mrs. Charles A. "The Old Mill," <u>The Story of Minnesota Lake</u>. Minnesota Lake, Minnesota: Centennial Committee, 1966.

Carley, Kenneth. <u>The Sioux Uprising of 1862</u>. St.Paul: Minnesota Historical Society, 1976.

City of Mankato. Community Calendar, 1984.

Crawford, Sherry. ed. <u>Chronicles of A Century: A 100 Year Look at Events that Shaped the History of Blue Earth and Nicollet Counties from 1900-1999</u>. Mankato, Minnesota: The Free Press, Co., 1999.

<u>History of Century Businesses and Churches</u>, 4 May, 1988.

Hughes, Thomas. "Steamboating on the Minnesota River." <u>Minnesota Historical Society Collections</u>. 10, part 1.

Krohn, Tim. "Resort Didn't Spring: 19th Century Plans Envisioned a Resort Based on Mineral Springs," <u>The Free Press</u>. (Mankato, Minnesota). fall, 2001.

Krohn, Tim. "Tragedies Mark Time: Mankato's History is Also Defined by Sour Moments in History." <u>The Free Press</u>. (Mankato, Minnesota). 26 January 2002.

Kunhardt, Dorothy Meserve and Philip B. Kunhardt Jr. <u>Twenty Days: A Narrative in Text and Pictures of the Assassination of Abraham Lincoln and the Twenty Days and Nights that Followed—The Nation in Mourning, The Long Trip Home to Springfield</u>. Foreword by Bruce Catton. North Hollywood, California: NewCastle Publishing Co., Inc., 1985.

Lagerquist, Mike. ed. <u>The History of North Mankato: Updated in 1998 Upon the City's 100th Anniversary</u>. North Mankato, Minnesota: City of North Mankato, 1998.

Leidner, Gordon. <u>Abraham Lincoln: The Complete Book of Facts, Quizzes & Trivia</u>. Shippensburg, Pennsylvania: Burd Street Press, 2001.

Lundin, Vernard E. At the Bend in the River: An Illustrated History of Mankato and North Mankato. Chatsworth, California: Windsor Publications, Inc., 1990.

Mankato City Directories: 1902, 1950.

Mankato Free Press. (Mankato, Minnesota). 21 August, 1908.
Mankato Free Press. (Mankato, Minnesota). 25 June, 1910.
Mankato Free Press. (Mankato, Minnesota). 25 October, 1929.
Mankato Free Press. (Mankato, Minnesota). 20 October, 1942.
Mankato Free Press. (Mankato, Minnesota). 27 June, 1952.
Mankato Free Press. (Mankato, Minnesota). 3 December, 1962.
Mankato Free Press. (Mankato, Minnesota). 15 February, 1963.
Mankato Free Press. (Mankato, Minnesota). 6 December, 1975.
Mankato Free Press. (Mankato, Minnesota). 26 May, 1978.
Mankato Free Press. (Mankato, Minnesota). 28 July, 1983.
Mankato Free Press. (Mankato, Minnesota). 12 April, 1984.
Mankato Free Press. (Mankato, Minnesota). 31 December, 1985.
Mankato Free Press. (Mankato, Minnesota). 30 June, 1988.
Mankato Free Press. (Mankato, Minnesota). 4 January, 1989.
Mankato Free Press. (Mankato, Minnesota). 15 February, 1989.
Mankato Free Press. (Mankato, Minnesota). 29 March, 1989.
Mankato Free Press. (Mankato, Minnesota). 29 December, 1989.
Mankato Free Press. (Mankato, Minnesota). 21 April, 1990.
Mankato Free Press. (Mankato, Minnesota). 11 July, 1992.
Mankato Free Press. (Mankato, Minnesota). 31 May, 1993.
Mankato Free Press. (Mankato, Minnesota). 18 September, 1993.
Mankato Free Press. (Mankato, Minnesota). 20 June, 1994.
Mankato Free Press. (Mankato, Minnesota). 22 August, 1994.
Mankato Free Press. (Mankato, Minnesota). 21 November, 1994.
Mankato Free Press. (Mankato, Minnesota). Special Edition. February, 1995.
Mankato Free Press. (Mankato, Minnesota). 17 June, 1995.
Mankato Free Press. (Mankato, Minnesota). 2 September, 1995.
Mankato Free Press. (Mankato, Minnesota). 31 July, 1996.

Mankato, Its First Fifty Years. 1852-1902. Containing Addresses, Historic Papers and Brief Biographies of Early Settlers and Active Upbuilders of the City. Prepared for the 50th Anniversary of the Settlement of Mankato. Mankato, Minnesota: Free Press Printing Co., 1903.

Neill, Edward D. and Charles S. Bryant. History of the Minnesota Valley, Including the Explorers and Pioneers of Minnesota and History of the Sioux Massacre. Minneapolis: North Star Publishing Company, 1882.

Restaurant Magazine. May, 1946.

Schrader, Julie Hiller. ed. The Heritage of Blue Earth County Minnesota. Dallas, Texas: Curtis Media Corporation, 1990.

Schrader, Julie A. History of the Red Jacket Valley. Mankato, Minnesota: Minnesota Heritage Publishing, 2001.

Stenzel, Edward M. Personal Recollections to his son, Bryce O. Stenzel. Mankato, Minnesota.

The Free Press, (Mankato, Minnesota). 10 March, 2001.

The Free Press, (Mankato, Minnesota). 23 February, 2002.

The Year of the Sesquicentennial: 150 Years Mankato Area. commemorative timeline. Taylor Corporation, 2002.

Ulrich, Mabel. John G. Rockwell and Parker T. Van de Mark. Minnesota County Histories Series: Blue Earth County. Minnesota Federal Writers' Project, 1938.

Upham, Warren. Minnesota Geographic Names: Their Origin and Historic Significance. St. Paul: Minnesota Historical Society, 1920. reprint ed., 1969.

Website. www.ci.mankato.mn.us City of Mankato, 2002.

Website. www.historicpanoramicmaps.com "The History of Panoramic Mapping."

Website. MSU Reporter (Betsy Alwin).

Whipple, Henry Benjamin. Lights and Shadows of a Long Episcopate: Being Reminiscences and Recollections of the Right Reverend Henry Benjamin Whipple, D.D., L.L. Bishop of Minnesota. With Portrait of the Author and Other Illustrations. New York: The Macmillan Company, 1889.

Wiecking, Anna. As We Once Were: Stories About the Settlement and Life of Blue Earth County From 1850 to the Early 1900's. Mankato, Minnesota: 1971.

Williams, J. Fletcher. With an Introduction by Lucile M. Kane. A History of the City of St. Paul to 1875. St. Paul: Minnesota Historical Society Press, 1983.

Acknowlegements

A special thank you to everyone who helped as I collected the material for this book. Thanks to the staff and volunteers of the Blue Earth County Historical Society and Marian Anderson, Dennis Dotson, Harley Goff, Brenda Lunz, Julie Schrader, Shelly Schulz, Arlene and Laurie Stenzel. Thanks also to everyone at Corporate Graphics who were involved with the printing of this book, especially Barb Wandersee and Richard Selle.

Photo Credits

Page viii	Historic Panoramic Maps & Photos, www.historicpanoramicmaps.com
Page xi, 9, 19, 22, 38, 64, 70, 93, 106	The Heritage of Blue Earth County, MN, Schrader
Page xii, 10, 20, 28, 46, 63, 69, 72, 76, 82, 109	Blue Earth County Historical Society
Page 26, 31-32, 34, 37, 40, 44, 49-50, 57-58, 60, 88, 94, 102, 110	Collection of Julie A. Schrader
Page 43	Horseless Carriage Gazette, Vol. 39, No. 1, Jan/Feb 1977
Page 82	John Cross
Page 84	Kelly Reuter
Page 99-100, 104	City of Mankato
Page 105	David A. Schrader
Page 110	Bryce O. Stenzel

Index

Able, Captain, 3
airport, 52, 55
Alexander, Paul "Lefty", 68
Alumni Plaza, 92
Allyn, Glen, 51
American Legion, 55, 74
American Legion Auxiliary, 51, 54
Anderson, Harvey, 60
Anderson, Marian, 96. See iii
Andrew Carnegie, 39
Andrews Opera Company, 61
Anthony Wayne, 3
Archer Daniels, 54
Armistice Day Blizzard, 85
Armory, 42
Armstrong Hall, 80
Armstrong, Louis, 67
Babcock & Wilcox, 7
Bandwagon, 79
Barney, Mrs. Paul, 68
Basie, Count, 67
Beach Boys, 67
Bell, Al, 61
Belle Mar Mall, 80
Ben Pay Hotel, 55
Bengston, Claude, 71
Benjamin, Frank, 55
Bethany Lutheran College, 47, 49
Bethlehem Lutheran Church, 86
Bierbauer Brewery, 8, 9
Bierbauer, Jacob, 8, 9
Bierbauer, William, 8, 9
blacksmith shop, 42
Blake, George E., 54
Blakeslee Stadium, 80
Blue Earth County, 5, 6, 7, 13, 36, 66, 83, 89
Blue Earth County Agricultural Association, 8
Blue Earth County Courthouse, 26, 27, 34, 35, 38

Blue Earth County Fairgrounds, 8, 67
Blue Earth County Historical Society, 7, 15, 18, 23, 41, 61, 91
Blue Earth County Library, 35
Blue Earth County Road 90, 98
Blue Mounds State Park, 80
Boston Shoe Repairing, 72
Boy Scouts, 52, 55
Brandrup, J.R., 28
Brett's Department Store, 97
Brown, Arline, 103
Bryan, William Jennings, 48
Buffalo, 88, 89, 110
Bull Run, 16
Bunker Hill, 13
Burton Hotel, 91
Burton, W.G.A., 91
Butler, Charles, 97
Butler House, 95, 97
Butler Jr., Charles, 97
Cambria, 30
Cameron, Simon, 13
Camp Fire, 47
Camp Lincoln, 14
Camp Patterson, 56
Camp Release, 16
Cannon, James, 13
Capone, Al, 31, 53
Cargill. See iii
Carlson Craft, 68
Carlson Letter Service, 68
Carlson, William, 68
Carnegie Library, 41
Carver, 3
Cedar Haven Lutheran Home, 18
Celebration of Lights, 91
Centenary Methodist Church, 55
Centennial Student Union, 81
Charleston Harbor, 13
Chaska, 16

Chateau De Amour, 25
Chautauqua, 48
Cheyenne, 5
Cheyenne Indians, 5
Chicago World's Fair, 62
Chippewa Indians (see Ojibway)
Civil War, 11, 66
Claridge, Gary, 74
Clements, Frank, 97
Club Royal, 72
Colfax, Schyler, 29
Comfrey, 96
Continental Can Company, 67
Country Store, 80
Crawford Center, 74
Cray, Judge Lorin, 36, 112
Cray, Lulu, 36
Crehan, Sister Mary Joseph, 47
Cub Foods, 74
Cumming's Ferry, 10, 18
Currier, Mortimer, 97
Cut Nose, 17
Dackins, John, 28
Dairy Queen West, 56
Dakota Conflict, 4, 5, 7, 8, 11, 13, 89, 111. See xii
Dakota Indians, 5, 43, 111
Dakota Meadows, 97
Dakota Memorial, 110
DeMoreau, Louis, 4
Dewey, George, 64
Dewey, Gus, 80
Dewey, Thomas, 68
Dillinger, John, 30, 31
Diphtheria, 25
Dodd Road, 1
Dolostone, 6, 37, 88
Dotson Company, 65
Dotson Company, Inc, 42
Drew, John, 61
Duley, William, 14
Eastgate Shopping Mall, 80
Eberhart, Adolph, 47
Eberhart, Mrs. Clara, 67

117

Eberhart, Vincent, 67
Edwards, Clara, 52
Ellerbe building, 24, 100
Empire Store, 16
Enfield Building, 8
Episcopal Church, 55
Evans, Dave "Doc", 74
Everett, Marion, 84
Faribault, 14
Farmfest, 86
Favorite, 16. See xii
Featherstonhaugh, George, 4
fire engine, 18
First National Bank, 22, 24, 100. See iii
First Presbyterian Church, 7
Fischer Clothing Store, 81
Fischer, Lee, 81
Fletcher, Lafayette G.M., 7
Fletcher, May, 45
Flood of 1951, 70, 73
Flood of 1965, 80
Fort L'Huillier. See ix
Fort Ridgely, 13
Fort Snelling, 8, 12, 13. See xii
Fort Sumter, 13
Fowler & Pay, 7
Frank Mettler Bar, 56
Franklin School, 55, 56
Frederick, Marcel "Sal", 77
Frederick, Robert "Bob", 77
Free Press. See iv
Friends of the Minnesota Valley Regional Library. See ii
Frost, George, 28
Fuller, Hiram, 4
Gage Center A, 80
Gage Center B, 80
Gage, Professor George M., 15
Gamble-Skogmo, 80
Garden City, 8, 30
George E. Brett Dry Goods Store, 16
Gestures, 78
Gifford, Mr. and Mrs. Frank, 67
Gifford, Quentin, 67

Glenwood Cemetery, 23, 35, 43
Godfrey, 14, 16
Golias, Tony, 81
Good Counsel, 42, 47
Good Thunder, 23
Gorman, Briney, 60
Graif, John, 54
Graif, Matt J., 54
Grand Theatre, 72, See iv
Grant, U.S., 29
Grasshopper plague, 24
Great Depression, 41
Greece, 81
GreyHound Bus Depot, 29
Griebel, Charley, 28
Gullickson, Tedd, 87
Gunning, Frank, 8
Gus-Johnson Plaza, 90
Hanna, Sarah Jane, 7
Hanson, Bert, 85
Happy Chef, 79
Haskel, "Spike", 68
Hayes, Jim, 74
Hegley, Herman, 15
Held, Anna, 61
Henrietta, 36, 106, 109
Hensley, Clinton, 8
Hielscher, Dr. J.A., 54
Hielscher Hall, 54
Hielscher, Helen Hughes, 54
Highland Arena, 80
Highland Park, 13, 62
Highway 169, 62, 79, 98
Highway 22, 66, 98
Hilltop Florists, 42
Hilltop Shopping Center, 80
Himmelman, Edward, 91
Holiday Inn, 86
Holiday Inn Hotel, 76
Holly, Buddy, 75
Honeymead Products, 79
Hotel Heinrich, 91
Hubbard Flour Mill, 78
Hubbard Mill, 29, 42
Hubbard Milling. See iii
Hubbard Milling Company, 20, 23, 24, 68
Hubbard, R.D., 20, 23, 24, 29

Humphrey, Vice President Hubert, 77
Hutchinson, 17
Ibach Brewery, 79
Ibach, Joseph, 25
Immanuel Hospital, 42, 81, 92, 93
Immanuel Lutheran High School, 99
Immanuel-St. Joseph's Hospital, 81
Indian Lake, 98
Inkpaduta, 8
Intergovernmental Center, 102. See iv
Iron truss bridge, 24
J.C. Penney Store, 41
Jackson, Henry, 3, 4, 6. See ix
Jackson, Mrs. Henry (Angelina Bivens), 4
James, John, 4
James-Younger Gang, 22, 24
Janavaras, John, 95
Jefferson, Adam, 7
Jefferson Bend, 15
Jefferson Elementary School, 79
John Deere, 79
John Philip Sousa's Band, 61
Johnson, Curtis "Swede", 68
Johnson, Governor John A., 47
Johnson, Gus, 92, 93
Johnson, Mrs. Parsons King (Laura Bivens), 4
Johnson, Parsons King, 2, 4-6. See ix
Jolly Millers, 68
Julia, 15
Kasota, 6
Kasota stone quarries, 6
Kato Ballroom, 67, 71
Kato Entertainment Center, 67
Kennedy, John F., 79
Kern Bridge, 21
KEYC, 79
Kirby, Jerry "Rip", 74
Kirchner, Merian Lovelace, 84

118

Klimpel, Bob, 41
Klugherz, Tom, 80
Knights of Columbus, 55
Korean Memorial, 89
Korean War, 73
Kost Garage, 71
KYSM, 64, 66, 68
KYSM AM, 62
LaFond, Gene "Peewee", 68
Lake Shetek Massacre, 14
Lamm and Landkamer, 36
lamplighter, 29
Lamson, Nathan, 17
Landkamer's, 42
Le Ray Township, 33
Leas Schwickert Arts Pavilion, 97
Lee, General Robert E., 16
Leech, General Samuel, 6
Legionnaires' Disease, 97
LeSueur County, 6
LeSueur, Pierre Charles, 6. See ix
Lewis Eastgate Drug, 80
Lewis, Jerry Lee, 67
Lewis, Sinclair, 45, 51
Lieske, Shirley, 84
Lime Township, 83
Lincoln, Abraham, 12, 16, 29, 40, 43
Lincoln Elm tree, 89, 91
Lincoln Park, 30
Lincoln, President, 13, 14
Lincoln School, 54, 67
Lincoln Township, 83
Lindbergh Jr., Charles, 54
Little Crow, 17
Little Giant, 67
Lombardo, Guy, 51
Long Prairie, 7
Lorene, 106
Lorenz, Herman, 56
Lovelace Library Wing, 84
Lovelace, Maud Hart, 35, 84. See iii
Loyola, 24, 56, 99
Lulsdorff, Lora, 61
Lutes building, 56
Luverne, 80
Macbeth, Florence, 48, 61
Madison Avenue hill, 42

Madison East Mall, 81, 82. See iv
Madsen, Earl, 74
Madsen's Super Valu, 74
Mahowald, Frank J., 65, 69
Mahowald's Sporting Goods & Hardware, 69
mail service, 8
Main Street Bridge, 10, 12, 47, 70, 104. See iv
Majestic Theater, 42
Mankato Airport, 85
Mankato Area 77 Lancers Marching Band, 87, 99
Mankato Area Vocational Technical Institute, 68, 73
Mankato Baltics, 28
Mankato Brewing Company, 80
Mankato Brick and Tile Company, 42
Mankato Citizen's Telephone Company, 42
Mankato City, 15
Mankato City Bus, 82
Mankato City Hall, 29, 94, 97
Mankato Civic Center, 97, 100
Mankato Commercial College, 31
Mankato Cycle Company, 69
Mankato Daily Review, 112
Mankato East, 85, 99
Mankato Electric Traction Company, 30, 38, 39
Mankato Elk's Band, 55
Mankato Elk's Nature Center, 97
Mankato Fire Department, 12, 13
Mankato Free Press, 68
Mankato High School, 34, 35, 46, 67, 73, 83
Mankato House Hotel, 6, 14, 29
Mankato Ice Company, 41
Mankato Independent, 8
Mankato Intergovernmental Center, 96

Mankato Linseed Oil Company, 39
Mankato Mall, 76, 86, 91
Mankato Mineral Springs Company, 35
Mankato Municipal Band, 52
Mankato Normal School, 15, 50, 54, 81, 91
Mankato Opera House, 61
Mankato State College, 74, 78, 82, 83
Mankato State University, 86, 87, 96. See ii
Mankato Street Railway System, 30
Mankato Symphony Orchestra, 73
Mankato Teachers' College, 38, 71
Mankato Township, 59
Mankato West, 34, 73, 87, 99
Mankato-Kasota Stone, 7
Mapleton, 24, 66
Marigold Dairy, 74
Marigold Dixielanders, 74
Marketown Foods, 80
Marsh, George H., 7, 8
Marso, Bill, 54
Maxfield, George, 6
Mayer Brothers, 43, 65
Mayer, Louis, 42
Mayo Clinic, 17
Mayo, Dr. William, 17
McDonnell, Father Martin, 47
McElroy Center, 80
McPherson Township, 7
Mead, Billy, 27, 28
Memorial Field, 73
Memorial Library, 81
Meningitis, 97
Menton, Dale, 80
Michaels' Minstrels, 74
Midwest Wireless Civic Center, 24, 97, 100-103. See iii
Miller, Glenn, 67
Miller Ice Company, 53
Miller, Thomas, 88, 91

Minneapolis, 26
Minneopa, 23
Minneopa Falls, 40, 41, 105
Minneopa State Park, 40, 41, 62
Minnesota Heritage Publishing. See ii
Minnesota Historical Society, 17, 111
Minnesota Lake, 12
Minnesota National Guard, 80
Minnesota Pollution Control Agency, 79
Minnesota River Steamboats, 107
Minnesota State University, 12, 55, 98, 103. See iv
Minnesota Valley Area Boy Scout Council, 55
Minnesota Valley Natural Gas Co., 72
Minnesota Valley Railroad, 16
Minnesota Valley Railway Depot, 15
Minnesota Valley Regional Library, 76, 84, 86
Minnesota Vikings, 81
Mister Softee Ice Cream truck, 79
Moore, Douglas R., 74
Morris Hall, 81
Morse, Daniel, 33, 35
Mount Kato, 62
Mueller's Superway, 80
Nachbar, C.A., 61
National Citizens Bank Building, 54
National Youth Administration, 61
Native American, 88, 112. See iii
Neill, Reverend Edward D., 3
Neisen, Harry, 74
Neilsen, Neil, 52, 56
Newman Center, 89
Nicholas, Caroline, 84
Nicollet, 5
Nicollet, Joseph, 4

North Mankato, 39, 55, 61, 71, 73, 89, 99, 103
North Mankato Public School, 55
Northern States Power, 92
Northfield Bank, 21, 22
Nyquist Clothing Company, 72
Oasis Drive-Inn, 61, 63
Odd Fellows Building, 91
Ojibway Indians, 111
Olcott, Chauncy W., 61
Old East Mankato School, 36
Old Log School, 7
Old Main, 38, 49, 91. See iii
Old Main Annex, 92
Old Main Village Retirement Community, 91
Omaha Indians, 5
Omaha Railroad Roundhouse, 56
Opera House, 45
Orpheus Club, 48
Osterholm, Dr. Michael, 103
Ostrander Bell Tower, 92
Otoe Indians, 5
Ott, George, 61. See xi
Our Savior's Lutheran Church, 75
Owen, Amos, 88. See iv
Palmer, George, 23, 39
Palmer, George M., 24
Patterson L. Mercantile Co., 72
Pauline, Max, 42
Pay, W.H., 55
Pearl Harbor, 65
Pearson, William, 24
Peayer, George, 28
Performing Arts Center, 81
Piche, Maurice, 68
Pickford, Mary, 61
Pleasant Grove School, 54
Polio, 79
Pope, Dianne, 73
Pope, John, 16
Post Office, 36, 37, 95
Powell, Terry, 74
Powwow, 85
Prohibition, 78

Queen Frock's, 72
R.D. Hubbard House, 20, 23, 89, 91
Ramsey, Governor, 16
Ramsey, Governor Alexander, 13
Rapidan Dam, 44, 47
Rasmussen Business College, 91
Rasmussen Park, 95
Rasmussen Woods Park, 97
Reconciliation Park, 88, 89, 98, 110, 111
Red Cross, 46, 47
Red Jacket, 24
Red Jacket Bridge, 47
Red Jacket Trail, 98
Red Owl, 80
Reedfield, Nora, 48
Reuter, Kelly, 84
Richardson, J.P., 75
Ringling Brothers Circus, 29
River Hills Mall, 97. See iv
RiverBend Academy Charter School, 80, 103
Roberts, Harry, 28
Robertson, Colonel D.A., 4
Rolvaag, Governor Karl, 77
Roos, Albert, 28
Roos, Charles, 28
Roos, George, 28
Roosevelt, Eleanor, 51
Roosevelt School, 55
Ruttle's 50s Grill, 80
Ryan, Len, 74
Sacred Heart Home for Orphans, 47
Saulpaugh Hotel, 30, 31, 79, 86
Saulpaugh, Thomas, 30, 31
Schellbau, Bill, 28
Schmidt's Leather Store, 72
School Sisters of Notre Dame, 11
Schmidt, Gottlieb, 9
Schreyer, Lowell, 74
Schroeder, Robert, 83
Searing Hall, 73
Seitzer, John, 97
Seppman, Louis, 15
Seppman Mill, 15, 19

Shaubut, Henry, 6
Shostag, Gottlieb, 17
Shostag Windmill, 17
Sibley, Henry, 16, 17, 59. See xi
Sibley, Henry Hastings, 4, 13, 30
Sibley Mound, 4
Sibley Park, 5, 10, 14, 18, 38, 39, 51, 59, 63, 65, 80, 95. See xi
Sibley Park Zoo, 39, 59, 60
Singer Sewing Machine, 72
Sioux Indians (see Dakota)
Sivanich, Mark, 87
Skihaven, 62
Small Pox, 25
Snow, John, 47
South Bend, 7, 8
South Bend Township, 6
Southern Minnesota Stock and Fairgrounds, 30
Spirit Lake Massacre, 2
St. Joseph's Hospital, 36, 81
St. Paul, 4, 5, 6, 8, 17
St. Peter, 1, 96
St. Peter and Paul's Catholic Church, 7, 23. See iii
St. Peter and Paul's Catholic School, 24, 42, 55
Standard Brewing Company, 16, 41
Standard Oil Company, 97
Stanley Steamer, 36
State Theater. See iv
Steamboats, 107
Steinberg, Ron, 74
Stemig, Ellie, 74
Stenzel, Arlene, 85
Stenzel, Bryce, 85, 86, 87. See ii
Stenzel, Edward, 82, 85, 86
Stenzel, Laurie, 85, 87, 97
Stephenson Music Co., 72
Stewart Brickyard, 42
Stewart, William E., 42
Stock, Edwin, 87
Stoltzman, George, 78
street car, 30
streetcar barns, 71

Sunshine Boys, 68
Supermarkets, 78
Swenson's Photo Shop, 41
Taft, William Howard, 30, 31, 47, 112
Taylor Athletic Center, 103
Taylor, Glen, 101
Taylor Library, 103
Tempo, 80
Thayer, Frank, 36
Thompson, Mary Ann, 7
Tillisch Optometric Eye Parlor, 72
Tinkcom, James Ray, 25
Tinkcomville, 22, 25
Tourtellotte, Colonel John, 30
Tourtellotte Hospital, 30
Tourtellotte Park, 38
Town Theater. See iv
Traverse des Sioux, 8
Treaty of Mendota, 3
Treaty of Traverse des Sioux, 3
Truman, Harry, 64, 68
Tschida, Ron, 97
Tschida, Sharalyn, 97
U. S. Army Corps of Engineer's Flood Control Program, 89, 104
Ulrich's Home Appliances, 72
Union Depot, 32, 36, 45, 68
Union School, 7
University of Minnesota, 103
Urban Renewal, 83, 86
Valens, Ritchie, 75
Vernon Center, 85
Veterans of Foreign Wars, 55
Veterans' Memorial Bridge, 89, 91, 104
Vetter Stone Company, 7
Victory Highway, 68
Vietnam Veterans' Memorial, 89
Vietnam War, 80
Wakefield, Sarah, 16
Walgreen's, 80
Waseca Counties, 7
Waterson, Bruce, 80

West Mankato, 15
Western Telegraph, 15
Whipple, Henry, 14
Wickersham, Dr. Moses, 8
Wickersham, Jason F., 8
Wiecking, Anna, 112
Wilkinson, Morton S., 43
Willette, Nancy, 97
Williams, Daniel, 4
Wilson Campus School, 74, 87
Windmiller Hill, 39
Windmiller, Louise, 42
Windmiller, Oswald, 42
Windom, William, 43
Winnebago Indians, 7, 43
Winnebago Agency House, 7
Winter Carnival, 53, 57, 102, 103
Winter Warrior, 88, 110
Wise, John C., 112
Wiswell, James, 15
Wold, Donald, 86
Wood, Chuck, 28
Works Progress Administration, 59
World Plowing Contest, 83, 85
World War I, 7, 47, 54, 66
World War II, 41, 65, 66, 68, 71, 73
World War II Memorial, 89
Wykoff, Clyde, 61, 63
Y Barbershop, 41
Yaeger's Bridge, 24
Yankee, 3
YMCA, 29, 39, 41
YMCA Barbershop, 41
YWCA, 33, 36, 86

Other Books Available from Minnesota Heritage Publishing

The Heritage of Blue Earth County
by Julie A. Schrader

The History of the Red Jacket Valley
by Julie A. Schrader

Maud Hart Lovelace's Deep Valley
by Julie A. Schrader

German Immigration to the Minnesota River Valley Frontier
by Bryce O. Stenzel

For more information about these books
visit our website: www.mnheritage.com
or contact
Minnesota Heritage Publishing
205 Ledlie Lane Suite 125
Mankato, MN 56001